THE OAKWOOD LIBRARY OF HISTORY

THE
LYNTON & BARNSTAPLE RAILWAY
1895–1935

by
L.T. Catchpole

THE OAKWOOD PRESS

© Oakwood Press 1988

ISBN 0 85361 363 X

First published	March, 1936
Second Edition	July, 1936
Third Edition	January, 1937
Fourth Edition	September, 1949
Fifth Edition	June, 1954
Reprinted	April, 1960
Reprinted	February, 1963
Reprinted	January, 1968
Sixth Edition	October, 1972
Reprinted	January, 1977
Reprinted	June, 1980
Reprinted	February, 1983
Seventh Edition	March, 1988

Printed by Bocardo Press Ltd, Oxford

Published by
The OAKWOOD PRESS
P.O.Box 122, Headington, Oxford.

Contents

	Chronology	6
Chapter 1:	**First Thoughts** Coach Services – Early Railway Schemes – Narrow Gauge Line from Barnstaple – The Filleigh Scheme – Support for the Narrow Gauge	9
Chapter 2:	**Construction and Opening** The Bill – The Prospectus – Difficulties – Inspection – Opening	13
Chapter 3:	**Equipment** Locomotives – Rolling Stock – Permanent Way – Stations and Halts	21
Chapter 4:	**The Route Described** Pilton Yard – Chelfham Viaduct – Bratton Fleming – Engineering Difficulties – The Summit – Lynton	35
Chapter 5:	**The Early Years** Criticisms and Suggestions – Platform Gardens – Snowstorms – Dean Steep Landslide	43
Chapter 6:	**Progress** Enterprise of Mr Drewett – Ilfracombe–Lynton Traffic – Road Motor Feeder Service – New Halts – Death of Sir George Newnes – Pre-War Prosperity	49
Chapter 7:	**The Southern Railway** Acquisition – Improvements – Advertising – Lack of Local Support – A Forecast	55
Chapter 8:	**The Closing and Sale** The Last Run – Sale by Auction – Dissolution	59
Appendix I:	**Locomotive Working** With Tables of 20 runs (*by Frank E. Box*)	65
Appendix II:	**Principle Lengths of Station Trackwork, etc.**	71
Appendix III:	**Monthly Engine Mileage, 1924 to 1928** (*compiled by W.E. Hayward*)	72
Appendix IV:	**Stores Issue Book Quantities (*coal and oil*) 1909, 1921, 1930 to 1934** (*compiled by W.E. Hayward*)	80
Appendix V:	**Traffic Reports 1901–1913**	84

Railway Clearing House Map of the Lynton and Barnstaple Railway showing associated railways.

Foreword to the 1988 Edition

When the last edition of this now definitive work on the Lynton and Barnstaple Railway went out of print, it was decided to produce a "new enlarged revised edition" as a tribute to the late L.T. Catchpole. This has been achieved by using more photographs, documents and ephemera which had been collected by the author during his lifetime's study of this fascinating railway.

The Oakwood Press hope you will agree that the choice of photographs and new additions make this (the thirteenth issue of the book) worthy of a place within your railway library.

Colin Judge, 1988

4

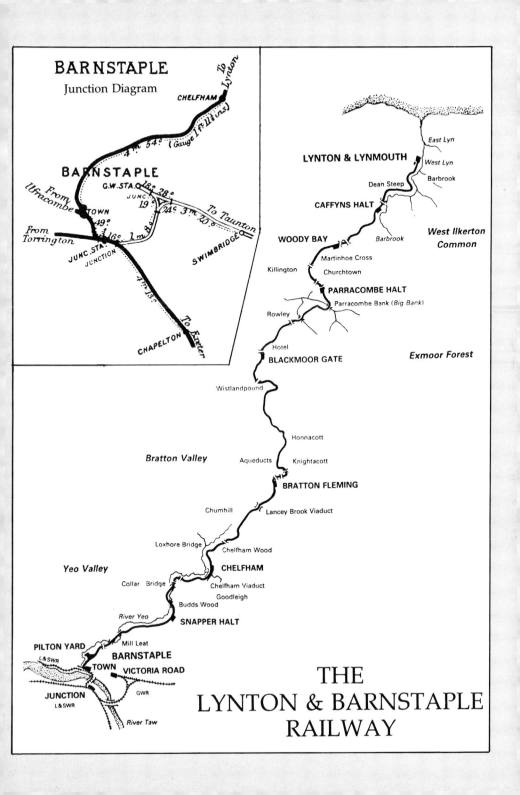

Chronology

1879   The Bill launched for a railway from Lynton connecting with the Devon & Somerset Railway at South Molton.

1883   Barnstaple & Lynton Railway Bill published. Not progressed.

1884   Promotion of a line from Lynton to Filleigh (on the GWR Barnstaple to Taunton line).

1885   The Lynton Railway Act introduced, covering Filleigh to Blackmoor Gate.

1886   Blackmoor Gate to Lynton extension Act.

1887   Act for branch – Blackmoor Gate to Combe Martin.

1890   New Act abandoning all but the Lynton to Blackmoor section. The Lynton and Lynmouth funicular cliff railway and hydro-electric plant on East Lyn River opened, sponsored by Sir George Newnes.

1892   Bill promoted for a tramway from Braunton to Blackmoor Gate to link with the Lynton and Blackmoor line, to be called "The Barnstaple & Lynton Electric Tramroad Co."

1894   25th September. Powers under the 1890 Act lapsed. Public meeting held during the summer proposing narrow-gauge line from Barnstaple to Lynton, plus the promotion of a standard-gauge line from Filleigh to Lynton.

1895   19th March. House of Lords considered both schemes, approving the Lynton & Barnstaple Bill, but rejecting the Filleigh scheme.
       27th June. Lynton & Barnstaple Railway Bill received Royal Assent.
       28th June. First Lynton and Barnstaple Railway board meeting, with Sir George Newnes as Chairman.
       17th September. First sod cut by Lady Newnes on the site of Lynton station.

1896   5th March. The tender of £42,100 from Mr James Nuttall (contractor) accepted by the Board of directors.
       24th September. Draft agreement with LSWR for use of Barnstaple Town station. (30 years lease)
       November. Tender for locomotives from Manning, Wardle & Co. of Leeds accepted.

1897   24th February. Board revealed that contractor had asked for an extension to 1st July, 1897 to complete work. This was refused.
       18th October. Meeting between Board, Consulting Engineer and Mr Nuttall, junr., who promised completion by 1st January, 1898.

1898   14th March. First train of one coach with locomotive *Taw* ran from Barnstaple to Lynton.
       16th March. Locomotive *Yeo* and two coaches travelled whole of the line carrying a press party.
       Board of Trade Inspection carried out during the month of May.
       11th May. Official opening ceremony.

1898 Line opened for general traffic on the 16th May.
June. Change the name of Bratton station to Bratton Fleming station.
July. Locomotive *Lyn* into service.

1899 1st May. Mr Drewett employed as Traffic Manager.
July. Parracombe Halt first appeared in timetable.
November. Mr Drewett appointed to Secretary and General Manager.

1901 The name of Wooda Bay station changed to Woody Bay.

1902 Platform wagons Nos. 20 and 21 into service.

1903 First railway motor coach service run by Sir George Newnes between Ilfracombe and Blackmoor during Summer.
Coach No. 17 and wagon No. 22 added to stock.
Snapper Halt opened.

1907 Caffyns Halt opened.

1909 Goods brake van No. 23 built at Pilton yard.

1910 9th June. Sir Thomas Hewitt, K.C. appointed due to Sir George Newnes' death.

1913 26th March. Two men killed in accident on ballast wagon.

1919 Sir Thomas Hewitt resigned as Chairman and succeeded by Col. E.B. Jeune.

1922 23rd June. Agreement reached for the line to be absorbed by LSWR.

1923 1st July. The Lynton & Barnstaple Railway Co. ceased to exist as an independent company, now under Southern Railway.

1925 July. Locomotive *Lew* entered traffic.

1926 Two cranes purchased secondhand. Coaches Nos. 3 & 4 converted to third class seating layout.

1927 Match truck built by the SR for the cranes. Operating loss of £5,900 reported.

1932 Loop at Bratton Fleming station removed.
The fitting of steam heating to the locomotives and some of the coaches.

1935 11th April. Meeting at Barnstaple, re-the continuation of the railway service.
29th September. The last train ran.
8th November. Removing the track from Lynton to milepost 15½ completed by the Southern Railway.
15th November. Sale of rolling stock, line and all equipment.

1936 Dismantling finished. Locomotive *Lew* overhauled and sold to Brazil.

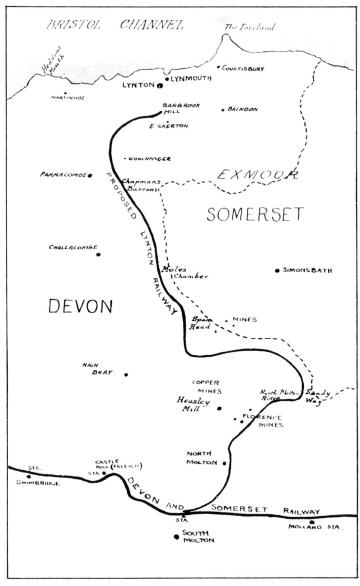

The First Projected Standard Gauge Railway to Lynton.

Chapter One
First Thoughts

Exmoor has maintained for centuries a fine natural wildness in spite of many attempts to violate its lonely expansiveness, and it furnishes, therefore, more ready material for the talents of poet and sportsman than for those of the railway prospector. Transport being in such little demand, it was in fact one of the last districts of England to adopt the wheeled vehicle, the pack horse and sledge sufficing until the close of the seventeenth century. Until the advent of tourism Combe Martin, Lynmouth and Porlock were only villages, having no great need of communication with each other or with the moorland hamlets that depended upon grazing for their precarious livings, and the development of coach services in this sparsely-populated neighbourhood was retarded also by the natural obstacle of Exmoor itself. With the opening of the Bristol & Exeter Railway in 1841 a service was instituted between Bridgwater and Minehead, which was extended to and from Lynton during the summer early in the '50s. In 1862 it ran from Williton and from Minehead in 1874, but during the summer only. The growth of Barnstaple as the "capital" of North Devon was also the means of introducing large numbers of people to the fine Exmoor scenery and climate, although Barnstaple itself lay beyond the western extremity of the moor. By 1860 excellent coach services were runing between Barnstaple and Ilfracombe, Combe Martin, and Lynton; the "highlands" of Exmoor, however, discouraged the coastal route and enabled the indirect approach to Lynton *via* Barnstaple — reached by rail in 1854 — to hold its own.

The old pack-horse road between Barnstaple and Lynton, with its many long single-figure gradients, was quite unsuitable for the operation of an efficient coach service; consequently several alterations and diversions were undertaken at various times, the new lengths for the most part following valleys instead of ridges.

In 1880, six years after the opening of the Ilfracombe railway, the service consisted of two coaches each way daily, the 20-seater, four-horse coaches *Tantivy* and *Glen Lyn* covering the 18 miles in 2 hours 50 minutes; the route was *via* Loxhore, where horses were changed and where, as at Parracombe, a fifth horse was required for the ascent of the steep hill. The fares between Lynton and Barnstaple were 5s. 6d. single and 7s. return. The running of this service is of particular interest in that the popular coach driver, Mr J. Baker, became station-master at Chelfham when the Lynton & Barnstaple Railway was opened in 1898.

The configuration of Exmoor does not lend itself to the easy construction of well-graded ways, either for road or rail, for the valleys are not only unfavourable in their direction, but they steepen excessively towards their upper ends so that they cannot be followed for any great distance. The building of the Devon & Somerset Railway from Taunton to Barnstaple (along the southern fringe of Exmoor) had tried to the utmost the skill of its engineer, while the Ilfracombe Railway involved long gradients of 1 in 40 and 1 in 36; even so, Ilfracombe station stands at about 200 feet above sea-level. There was, nevertheless, an insistent demand for a railway to serve Lynton and Lynmouth, the lovely twin villages whose fame was spreading rapidly far and wide, but the two companies expected to put up the necessary capital (the London & South-Western and Great Western Railways) declined on the grounds that the sparsely populated district could not produce sufficient revenue. There were also several independent proposals emanating from local residents, among which that of the Rev. H.S. Pinder, of Bratton Fleming, appeared in the 'seventies, favouring a coastal route from Ilfracombe *via* Combe Martin; but all such schemes were unable to obtain sufficient financial support. Lynton, however, had decided to become a recognised watering-place and, interesting itself in any proposal for a railway, it examined plans for railways from Ilfracombe, Barnstaple, and Castle Hill (Filleigh), one scheme proposing to follow the line of a disused mineral railway in the valley of the River Mole. In 1884 a line was suggested from Lynton to Barnstaple *via* Kentisbury, but in the following year the Devon & Somerset line was favoured again as the starting point, the Filleigh & Blackmoor Gate Railway proposing to surmount the high ground south of Lynton by way of High Bray and Challacombe. In the next year the company obtained powers to extend its line from Blackmoor to Combe Martin and to Lynton, but nothing was done towards actual construction. Then, after a lapse of six years, the company sought powers to build an additional line from Blackmoor to Barnstaple and to operate all its lines electrically, altering its name to "The Barnstaple & Lynton Electric Tramroad Company." Although the Bill passed the House of Lords it was not proceeded with in the subsequent Session, and no more was heard of this interesting scheme.

The lines so far proposed, from the nature of the country to be traversed, would have entailed a very high cost of construction with even a single line of railway, and this fact led certain influential gentlemen of Lynton to consider the possibility of building a narrow gauge railway from Barnstaple, the North Wales narrow-gauge lines being cited as successful examples; those who associated themselves with this scheme were Mr E.B. Jeune, The Manor House, Lynmouth; Mr Thomas Hewitt, The Hoe, Lynton; and Sir George Newnes, Bart., Hollerday Hill, Lynton. The gauge of 2 ft (1 ft 11½in.) was claimed to lower the cost of construction considerably, since the line would be able to follow the contours of the country with curves of five chains radius; but criticism was aroused at the mention of break-of-gauge disabilities at Barnstaple, for many West-countrymen had witnessed in former years the delays that had occurred at the meeting points of the broad and standard gauges. Estimates showed, however, that the anticipated traffic would be insufficient to pay interest on a standard-gauge line costing about £8,000 per mile to construct, whereas by the adoption of the narrow gauge, with an estimated construction cost of roughly £2,500 per mile, it was considered that the traffic would be sufficient to pay both the working expenses and interest on the capital. The inaccuracy of these estimates is shown by the fact that the construction cost of the narrow-gauge line proved to be £5,000 per mile, which might have been sufficient for the construction of a standard-gauge "light" railway. The "narrow" cause was further championed by the assertions that a 6-chain curve on a 2 ft gauge line was not more objectionable than a 12-chain curve on the standard gauge, while the fears of the break-of-gauge critics were allayed by the statement that coal and other water-borne traffic would be loaded direct into the Lynton company's trucks from the quay at Barnstaple.

Although the promoters of the narrow-gauge Lynton line now had the field to themselves as far as a direct line from Barnstaple was concerned, a rival scheme for a line to start from Filleigh was sponsored by the Great Western and received some support from Lynton residents. Numerous advantages from the engineering point of view also were claimed for the route. Mr Barlow, engineer to the Filleigh line, found that it would be more convenient to build the line along the ridges of hills than in the valleys, and he claimed to have discovered a route that would not involve the construction of cuttings, bridges, or engineering work of any magnitude in a distance of twelve miles; the construction cost would therefore be relatively low. The railway, of standard gauge, would have a double junction at Filleigh, the western arm being used by a local service between Barnstaple and Lynton, and the eastern arm by the Midland and London traffic. The total length of the line would be 16½ miles and the ruling grade 1 in 40. Undoubtedly this line had much in its favour, and, supported by a powerful company, it came within sight of success. It is safe to assert that if the promoters had obtained the backing of Sir George Newnes, whose popularity was then at its height, the narrow-gauge railway would not have been built, but that gentleman, having made up his mind on the matter, was not easily influenced. Shadows of doubt began to fall upon the prospects of the Filleigh scheme following a speech by its leading promoter, Viscount

Ebrington, in which certain inaccuracies crept into the enthusiastic discourse, and, since the misfortunes of the Devon & Somerset Railway shareholders were not forgotten, the company found it impossible to obtain the necessary goodwill. Lynton and Lynmouth inhabitants, however, favoured the narrow-gauge railway for many reasons, as may be seen from a brief account of a meeting held in Lynton in May 1895. Mr J. Heywood, Chairman, said:

> Gentlemen, this Meeting has been called to consider the question of the Railway Bill now in Parliament. We know that the Bill has been opposed tooth and nail by others, especially the Great Western Railway. Recently a letter appeared in a popular paper asking us to go for the Filleigh Scheme, but our minds are made up (*cheers*) and we feel sure that the passing of the Bill means that we shall have a railway (*loud cheers*). There have been other Bills, but each of them has been only a bogus scheme. We should support the present Bill for the following reasons: first, because this line will take us where we want to go; secondly, we believe it to be the only Honest Scheme; and thirdly, because its Directors have a local interest, as owners of property, in the progress of Lynton. (*Applause*).

A petition to the House of Commons in favour of the Lynton & Barnstaple Railway Bill was then read by the Chairman.

Sir George Newnes, Bart., Chairman, Lynton and Barnstaple Railway Co.

Chapter Two
Construction and Opening

The Lynton & Barnstaple Railway Bill received the Royal Assent on 27th June, 1895; it authorised a capital of £72,000 and a further borrowing powers of £23,300. The Directors were those gentlemen whose names have been given already, with the addition of Mr W.H. Halliday, who had been actively interested in the scheme since its inception by Sir George Newnes. Sir James Szlumper was appointed Consulting Engineer, and Mr C.E. Roberts Chanter, of Barnstaple, acted as Solicitor. The Company's offices were situated on Church Hill, Lynton; the Secretary was Mr F.B. Erridge. The Prospectus stated that the Company proposed "to construct and work a narrow-gauge Line of Railway, 19 miles 1 furlong 5 chains in length, from Barnstaple to Lynton, starting from a joint station with the L&SWR Co. within the town of Barnstaple, and terminating at Lynton." The five intermediate stations were to be placed near Chelfham Mills, Bratton Fleming, Blackmoor Gate, Parracombe, and Martinhoe Cross. There was no mention of Snapper Halt, but Parracombe was promised a station. "Martinhoe Cross" became Woody Bay, which in the Prospectus was spelt "Wooda Bay" and described as a "rising watering-place, where a pier is now being constructed."

Considerable excursion traffic was anticipated, for it was stated that "as many as thirty four-horse coaches and brakes enter Lynton every day in the season, heavily laden with passengers." As a large proportion of the excursionists came from Ilfracombe and not Barnstaple, however, this statement was rather misleading. "This traffic", the Prospectus continued, "will be increased by the pleasure of travelling on a line of the same nature as the famous Festiniog, Corris, and North Wales Narrow-Gauge Railways. It is the intention of the Directors to provide observation cars, so that perfect enjoyment of the scenery may be obtained. The narrowness of the permanent way will reduce the interference with the scenery to the lowest possible limits, and this was a great factor in determining the width of the gauge. The position of the station at Lynton has been chosen so that it will not be visible from Lynton or Lynmouth, and hence the beauties of the place will in no way be injured." No one will deny that the desired invisibility was successfully obtained, although at the price of inaccessibility, for the inconveniently situated terminus proved to be a great mistake.

The L&SWR agreed to give through bookings of passengers and goods over their line and "arranged to move their present Barnstaple Town station so as to have a joint station with the Lynton line, the former company agreeing to contribute £2,000 towards the cost of such joint station." The Lynton company negotiated with the Great Western Railway to obtain through bookings and favourable terms for through traffic, but it was not successful. The Town Council of

Barnstaple granted to the Lynton company a site for the new station and for ample quay accommodation on the River Yeo, so that sailing vessels of 200 tons could discharge direct into the company's trucks.

The Directors were optimistic regarding the average speed to be obtained on their line, for they stated that "the mails, which are now carried from Lynton to Barnstaple in three hours, will doubtless be handed over by the Post Office authorities to the railway, which can do the same service in an hour." Including the time for the journey between Lynton and its invisible terminus, however, two hours would have been a more accurate estimate; the running time alone would obviously exceed sixty minutes. The annual receipts were given as £12,800, but not much more than half this sum was realised in practice and the estimated working expenses were far below the actual figure.

The prospectus was no sooner issued than the whole of the capital was heavily over-subscribed. The ceremony of cutting the first sod was performed at Lynton by Lady Newnes on 17th September, 1895, the event being marked by processions and great rejoicing. The contract for construction was let to Mr J. Nuttall, of Manchester, who began work in March 1896, under the direction of Mr Frank W. Chanter (brother of C.E.R. Chanter), Resident Engineer to the Lynton & Barnstaple Railway Company.

Many unforseen difficulties now arose, both for the company and for the contractor. The former discovered that several landowners on the route were not as friendly as they had appeared to be, with the result that additional capital had to be raised to meet the cost of the land, descibed by Sir George Newnes as "extortionate"; there was opposition also from Barnstaple, where the company proposed to cross two busy streets upon the level despite its original intention to erect bridges, the excuse being that the cost would be excessive. Certain residents of the town deplored the loss of a picturesque but unsavoury piece of land known as Monkey Island which disappeared in the construction of the new Town station and North Walk, although more practical people regarded the new station as some compensation.

Opposition at Parracombe was dealt with by degrading its proposed station to a halt, at which, however, the company was obliged to stop all its trains, since a free supply of pure water for the locomotives was available there. Finally, some dissatisfaction was felt at Lynton with the site of the station, for the inhabitants naturally felt that their support of the line in its early stages was already forgotten by the company in placing the terminus 250 feet above the town; by continuing the line round the shoulder of a hill a much more favourable site could have been found at the foot of the old Barnstaple road, but oppostion from the owner of the required land made this impossible.

The chief of the difficulties which the contractor was facing were due to the nature of the ground to be excavated; it had been supposed that nothing more than ordinary soil existed along the route of the line, but in fact continuous blasting was necessary to remove the hard rock which was encountered. This miscalculation may in part be explained by the intention of the promoters to carry the railway along the surface of the ground as far as possible, but they had not realised that to obtain a formation along hill-sides where the natural slope averaged about 1 in 2½ a great amount of excavation would be involved. Further, the many side valleys or "combes" vastly increased the amount of cutting and filling, and the settling of the embankments was delayed by extaordinary wet weather, which at times caused work to be entirely suspended. It is difficult to believe that anyone, after more than a glance at the country, could fail to observe the outcrops of the rock along the path of the line, or would suppose that the depth of the soil was more than a few inches; but it was due to such carelessness as this that the line began its working life in adverse conditions.

These geological misapprehensions had cost the contractor an additional £22,000, nearly half the total estimated cost of construction; the price of land and compensation was found to be *four times* the estimated figure. It was regrettable that the company's consulting engineer should have been responsible for so many great inaccuracies; under his authority the company had stated that "the cost of construction would not exceed the sum of £50,000, the line contained no works of any great magnitude, being almost altogether a surface line, would be open for traffic in the summer of 1897, and be completed and equipped without entrenching on the Company's borrowing powers. The journey from Barnstaple to Lynton will be done in the hour." Not one of these statements proved to be even approximately accurate, and his action in awarding to Mr Nutall the sum of £27,000 for blasting and extra work – against the terms of the contract – was indeed unfortunate, resulting in the permanent crippling of the railway company's finances. A final calamity occurred in the bankruptcy of the contractor, for although the Court of Appeal gave its verdict for the company, the financial position of the contractor prevented it fromrecovering costs. Further, it had to complete the construction of the line, and in addition lost the benefit of a clause in the agreement which had provided that the contractor was to maintain the permanent way for one year after completion. Under the heading of "Nothing for Nuttall" *The North Devon Herald* made the following comments on the case:

> There can be no doubt that the decision of the Appeal Court *in re* Nuttall
> *v.* Lynton & Barnstaple Railway Company is a just one, and however hard

the result may be upon the plaintiff, who was the contractor, the Company has won fairly and squarely all through the litigation. Five judges have now given it as their opinion – two in the Divisional and three in the Appeal Court – and Sir James Szlumper, the arbitrator, was altogether wrong in awarding a sum of money to Mr Nuttall, because he had to do some extra unexpected work in building the line. It was Mr Nuttall's business to find out beforehand what he had to do, and then to make his charges for doing it. Instead of this, however, the contractor bound himself by a solemn agreement to carry out the contract for better or for worse – unfortunately for him it proved to be worse. Having to his astonishment to excavate rock instead of clay, he sought to go behind a special clause in the agrrement which explicitly stated that there were to be no "extras" and demanded an extra payment of about £27,000, which the arbitrator, Sir James Szlumper, promptly awarded him. The reversal of this award by the Divisional Court, and the confirmation of such reversal by the Appeal Court, may possibly open up the all-important question of arbitration, and throw a slur upon it which it certainly does not deserve; this, of course, would be most regrettable, but, so far as the question of the Lynton & Barnstaple Railway Company's position is concerned, there cannot be two opinions as to the justice of the decision arrived at. Let us hope that the decision will be accepted as absolutely final, for nothing would be gained by any further appeal.

The contractor is known to have used three locomotives in the construction of the line, with the possibility of more. The best known and photographed was an 0–4–2ST locomotive named *Excelsior* built by W.G. Bagnall of Stafford in 1888 (Works No. 970). She was built for the Kerry Tramway (Mid-Wales) and sold in 1895 to Nuttall's before being transferred to the Lynton and Barnstaple Contractors. The locomotive only weighed 2¾ tons (working) but developed a tractive effort of 1,290 lb, gauge 1 ft 11½ in. with 5 in. x 7½ in. outside cylinders. Her last days were spent on the Portland Tramways moving stone.

The second locomotive was a 0–4–0ST named *Slave* but further evidence of its origin and makers cannot be found but in a sale on the 6th January, 1899 quoted, "a locomotive 0–4–0ST with 5 in. x 10 in. O.C. was offered ex Lynton and Barnstaple Railway". This could have been this locomotive, whereas the other 0–4–0ST (nicknamed unofficially *Kilmarnock*) was built by Andrew Barclay of Kilmarnock in 1892 and not disposed of until after March 1900 as records show that the directors instructed that it should be "sold for £120 or to the best advantage".

The line was ready for the Board of Trade inspection which took place in May 1898. The party consisted of Col. Yorke (of the Board), Sir James Szlumper, Mr Frank Chanter, and the unfortunate Mr Nuttall. The inspection was extremely thorough, beginning at 10 am and finishing at 7 pm, and all the bridges were tested with two

Lady Newnes cutting the first sod on the site of the Lynton Goods Yard, on the 1st September, 1895.   *Author's collection*

Sir George Newnes receiving the Mayor and his party at Barnstaple Town for the opening ceremony on the 11th May, 1898.   *Author's collection*

Contractor's locomotive *Excelsior* built by Bagnalls and (*right*) a further locomotive used by contractor Nuttall during the construction stage, this time built by Barclay's.   *Author's collection*

The single line over Chelfham Viaduct as viewed from the Barnstaple side showing the almost 90° bend in the track that approached the viaduct.

Author's collection

Navvies working on track construction during the building of the Railway.
Author's collection

A fine old photograph taken on the opening day of the railway showing two of the locomotives and coaching stock at Pilton Yard depot on 11th May, 1898.
Author's collection

The opening scene of the railway at Lynton. *Author's collection*

Lady Newnes cutting the ribbon on the occasion of the arrival of the first train at Lynton Station. *Author's collection*

Lynton and Barnstaple Railway staff seen here outside the shed at Pilton Yard in 1911. Mr Charles Drewett (General Manager) in the centre of the second row. *Author's collection*

Cover of the first Lynton and Barnstaple Railway Timetable of May 1898.

LYNTON AND BARNSTAPLE RAILWAY.

LOCAL SERVICE between BARNSTAPLE AND LYNTON, and *vice versa.*

ALL TRAINS PARLIAMENTARY

DOWN.—Week Days.		a.m.		a.m.		a.m.		p.m.		p.m.		Sundays	a.m.	
Barnstaple (Town)	... dep.	6 35	...	8 40	...	11 30	...	3 45	...	5 24	...		7 30	...
Chelfham	"	7 1	...	9 9	...	11 52	...	4 8	...	5 47	...		7 54	...
Bratton	"	7 20	...	9 25	...	12 9	...	4 27	...	6 3	...		8 15	...
Blackmoor	"	7 45	...	9 50	...	12 31	...	4 49	...	6 25	...		8 40	...
Woody Bay	"	8 9	...	10 11	...	12 53	...	5 10	...	6 49	...		9 4	...
Lynton	arr.	8 25	...	10 25	...	1 9	...	5 25	...	7 5	...		9 20	...

UP.—Week Days.		a.m.		a.m.		p.m.		p.m.		p.m.		Sundays	p.m.	
Lynton	... dep.	6 14	...	9 10	...	1 50	...	3 25	...	5 45	...		5 38	...
Woody Bay	"	6 33	...	9 25	...	2 3	...	3 43	...	6 3	...		5 57	...
Blackmoor	"	6 56	...	9 53	...	2 31	...	4 6	...	6 28	...		6 22	...
Bratton	"	7 23	...	10 15	...	2 53	...	4 31	...	6 50	...		6 47	...
Chelfham	"	7 40	...	10 29	...	3 8	...	4 46	...	7 5	...		7 4	...
Barnstaple (Town)	arr.	8 2	...	10 50	...	3 30	...	5 7	...	7 26	...		7 26	...

The first timetable train service on the line.

locomotives. The result was entirely favourable, which was most creditable, in view of the obstacles met with during construction. A trial trip was run before the public opening; but it was marred by the train's refusal to proceed beyond Woody Bay, due to overloading the four coaches. This, necessitated the journey being completed ignominiously in such road vehicles as could be obtained locally. On arriving at Lynton the party was entertained at the Valley of Rocks Hotel.

The railway was declared open to the public on Wedneday 11th May, 1898, by Sir George and Lady Newnes, amid scenes of great festivity, large crowds gathering at the stations to welcome the first train, which, of course, was gaily decorated with flags, while Lynton itself was filled with banners and emblems of goodwill. Strange scenes were often witnessed at the opening of a railway; on this occasion, for example, the signals at Lynton station were almost obscured by enthusiastic life-boat men (in full life-saving attire) who had climbed the signal posts so as to obtain a better point of vantage.

Details of the first trains were recorded as follows:

Barnstaple Town	dep.	11.15 am	Driver Lodge
Barnstaple Yard	pass	11.18 am	Fireman Glover
Chelfham	pass	11.40 am	Guard Glover
Bratton	arr.	11.55 am	Carriages 6,4 and 2
		Water if necessary	
	dep.	12.05 pm	
Blackmoor	pass	12.25 pm	
Wooda Bay	pass	12.44 pm	
Lynton	arr.	1.00 pm	

On arrival at Lynton, engine will halt short of ribbon, and then advance to end of platform when same is cut. The engine and train will remain at Platform No. 1 until after the arrival of the second train. Both will probably have to go to Wooda Bay for water. The second train will leave Barnstaple Town at 11.40 pm as per following timetable:

Barnstaple Town	dep.	11.40 am	Driver Pilkington
Barnstaple Yard	pass	11.43 am	Fireman Willis
Chelfham	pass	12.01 pm	Guard Pargeter
Bratton	pass	12.25 pm	Carriages 5,3 and 1
Blackmoor	pass	12.45 pm	
Wooda Bay	pass	1.05 pm	
Lynton	arr.	1.20 pm	

This train will run into the bay at Lynton. As soon as platforms are clear of passengers, the train must be shunted ready for the return journeys with carriages No. 1 and No. 2 at rear, and on returning Driver Pilkington will start first with the train that Driver Lodge took up. First return train:

Lynton	dep.	5.20 pm
Wooda Bay	pass	5.37 pm
Blackmoor	pass	6.00 pm
Bratton	pass	6.22 pm
Chelfham	pass	6.37 pm
Barnstaple Yard	pass	6.57 pm
Barnstaple Town	arr.	7.00 pm

Driver to run round train and take it to yard. Signalman Masters to note that second train must not leave Chelfham until first train is safe in yard.

Driver Lodge will leave Lynton with the train that arrived second at 5.45 pm and will run as per the following times:

Lynton	dep.	5.45 pm
Wooda Bay	pass	6.01 pm
Blackmoor	pass	6.22 pm
Bratton	pass	6.46 pm
Chelfham	pass	7.06 pm
Barnstaple Town	arr.	7.27 pm

All carriages required must be taken by the engine two at a time by 9 am in the following order – Yard 6, 4, 2, 5, 3, 1 – Town station, so that the second engine can go back to Town station light and stand in Dock Road until first train has gone away, and then back on to 5, 3, 1 ready to start.

All signals necessary must be worked by Station-master. Gateman Bray to be on duty at Braunton Road, and Signalman Masters at Pilton Bridge Box.

Foreman Fitter Pearce to see that all coaches are well oiled and doors of carriages locked.

In performing the opening ceremony at the station, Sir George said they were allowing 1 hr 40 min because of the newness of the permanent way. The first train was hauled by the locomotive *Yeo*, and subsequently commemorative medals were presented to all primary schoolchildren. A triumphal arch greeted it at Bratton station, where the Parish Council presented an address to Sir George Newnes. The first train arrived at 1.17 pm at Lynton station where it stopped just short of the station to allow Lady Newnes to alight and cut the ribbons across the track.

The line was finally opened to general traffic on 16th May with the first train leaving at 8.49 am.

Alas, the glamour that had accompanied the opening ceremonies soon gave way to criticism, a change of opinion encountered by railways of all gauges at all times. The trains were painfully slow – the carriages rolled alarmingly – Lynton station was absurdly inaccessible – these were some of the complaints received by the company which was labouring under the greatest difficulties in its honest endeavour to give the line a fair start. But the financial position had been permanently damaged by the excessive cost of construction (the legal and Parliamentary expenses alone had exceeded the amount spent upon the purchase of engines, carriages, and wagons), and the raising of additional capital until the figure stood at £127,268, although necessary, made the prospect of paying a dividend even more remote than ever.

During the summer of 1898 an enquiry was held at Minehead, before the Light Railway Commissioners, for the purpose of hearing the case put forward by the promoters of a coastal line known as the Minehead & Lynmouth Light Railway. A summary of the Enquiry was reported in the *West Somerset Free Press* of 13th August, 1898, as follows: "Proposal for a 2ft gauge railway from Minehead adjoining GWR terminus to Lynmouth; estimated cost, £87,000. The promoters were some of the Directors of the Barry Railway. It was really a South Wales scheme to bring excursionists by boat from Cardiff to Minehead and then rail to Lynmouth. Distance, Minehead to Lynmouth 20 miles 3 furlongs. The steepest gradient proposed was 1 in 40. The only local supporter of standing was Mr G.F. Luttrell of Dunster Castle, who was a large owner of property in and about Minehead. The Engineer was Sir James Szlumper, who had been Consulting Engineer of the Lynton and Barnstaple Railway.

After sitting for one day only the Commissioners stated on the following morning that they saw no reason for prolonging the Enquiry; they could not recommend that compulsory powers should be excercised for the acquisition of land. It was purely a line for tourist traffic and would not help agricultural interests in the district."

 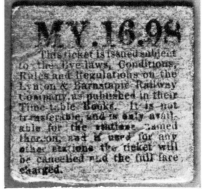

Reproduction of the first ticket issued.

Chapter Three
Equipment

It must be agreed that the equipment of the line was far above the average for any similar type of railway. The signalling apparatus was supplied by Evans, O'Donnell & Co., with Tyer's automatic tablet instruments. All points and signals were interlocked, but distant signals were not installed. The locomotive stock at the opening consisted of three 2–6–2 side tank engines constructed by Messrs Manning, Wardle & Co., of Leeds, their main features being:

Weight in working order	27¼ tons
Cylinders (two)	10½ in. by 16 in.
Coupled wheels	2 ft 9 in.
Pony and trailing wheels	2 ft
Total wheelbase	17 ft 9 in.
Rigid wheelbase	6 ft 6 in.
Working pressure	160 lbs per sq. in.
Capacity of tanks	550 gallons
Heating surface	383 sq. ft
Length overall	27 ft
Width over platform	6 ft 7 in.
Water tank capacity	550 gallons

The maker's numbers and the names given to them by the company were 1361 *Yeo*, 1362 *Exe*, and 1363 *Taw*.

During the first year of operation it was found that a fourth engine would be required, and, since there was at that time an engineering strike in this country, an order was placed with the Baldwin Locomotive Works, Philadelphia, USA, who built and delivered a 2–4–2 tank locomotive at extremely short notice. It bore the maker's number 15,965, and was given the name *Lyn*, though to the staff it was always known as "Yankee". Partly, no doubt, because its American taste and habits were not fully understood, it came to be looked on with some suspicion by drivers and fitters, who certainly expended more care on it than would have been its lot in the States. In its favour it should

Line drawings of the maker's plate and the smokebox doorplate on the American built Locomotive *Lyn*.   *Courtesy Mr R.E. Tustin*

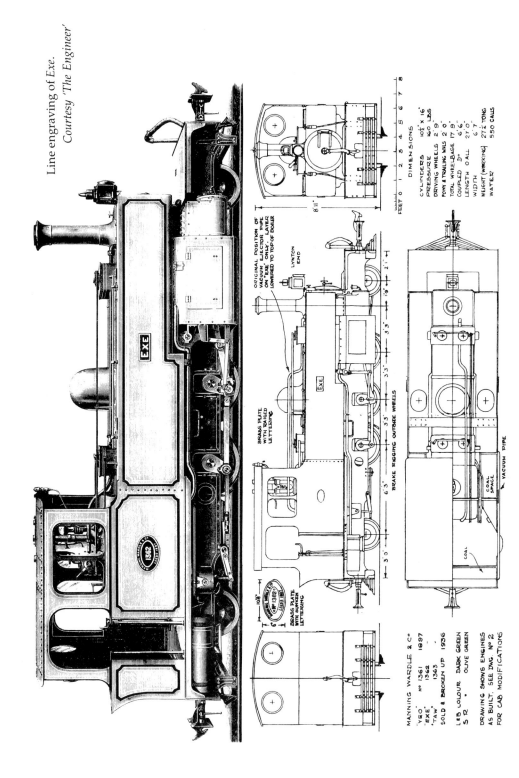

Line engraving of Exe.
Courtesy 'The Engineer'

Courtesy, Hunslet (Holdings) PLC

Official works drawing from Manning Wardles of Order No. 39800 for the three engines No. 1361 *Yeo*, No. 1362 *Exe* and No. 1363 *Taw*.

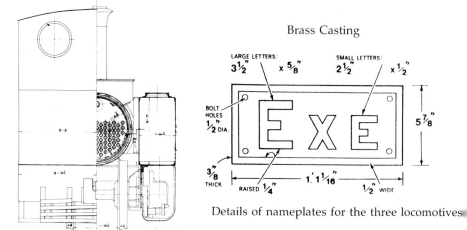

Details of nameplates for the three locomotives

Cross-section of locomotive and end details.

be said that it possessed a greater freedom on curves, due to a rigid wheelbase of only 5 ft. Other dimensions differing from those of the six-coupled locomotives were:

Weight in working order..................	22 tons.
Cylinders (two)............................	10 in. by 16 in.
Total wheelbase	17 ft 7 in.
Rigid wheelbase...........................	5 ft 0 in.
Working pressure..........................	180 lbs per sq.in.
Capacity of tanks..........................	800 US gallons
Heating surface............................	379 sq.ft
Length overall	28 ft
Width over platform	7 ft 2 in.
	(6 ft 7 in. over the tanks and cab)

Overall height...............................	8 ft 11 in.
Tractive effort @ 85% WP...............	7418 lb
Main Wheels dia.	2 ft 9 in.
Pony truck dia.	1 ft 10 in.
Water tank capacity	664 gallons

It was the only American-built engine to run on the Southern Railway, and it was the only one to have bar frames.

A fine view of the two Manning Wardles in Southern livery, *Lew* and *Exe* outside the Pilton sheds towards the last days of steam.

F. Box, Author's collection

No. 188 *Lew* in Southern Railway livery being prepared at Pilton shed for duty.

Author's collection

No. 188 *Lew* ready for the run to Lynton standing here at Barnstaple Town. This view shows the short safety valve with which the locomotive was originally fitted. *Real Photos: courtesy Ian Allan Ltd*

Another view of No. 188 *Lew* seen here at Woody Bay in 1935 (the wooden armed start signal already showing the right of way). A good view of the rear details of the locomotive and of wagon No. 28312.

Real Photos: courtesy Ian Allan Ltd

The actual official photograph sent to the Lynton and Barnstaple Railway by Baldwins of America, with the quotation for *Lyn*. The locomotive was painted in black with white painted name. *Author's collection*

A fine view of *Lyn* pre-1929, showing the nameplate in its original position before its overhaul at Eastleigh. *Author's collection*

A view of Blackmoor station with No. 762 *Lyn* taking water before pressing on to Lynton. A passenger is looking out on the wrong side obviously wondering why the hold up. *Author's collection*

A view of No. 762 *Lyn* outside Pilton Sheds. *Author's collection*

No. 762 *Lyn* returning from Eastleigh Works in 1929, after major overhaul
and repaint seen here in the trans-shipment sidings at Barnstaple.
Author's collection; Knight, Barnstaple

A fine view of *Lyn* and crew at Lynton station prior to the 1929 overhaul.
Author's collection

Two views of No. 761 *Taw*, one showing the Lynton and Barnstaple Railway
livery and the other the SR livery and lining.   *Author's collection*

Two views of No. 759. *Yeo,* again showing the different liveries of the Lynton & Barnstaple Railway and Southern Railway. The top view shows the locomotive at Woody Bay carrying the oval number plate on the rear with 759 number. The livery was SR olive green, lined in black and white and yellow (chrome) lettering. The bottom view shows the considerable amount of freight moved with the passenger service.   *Author's collection*

Two early views of *Exe* (No. 760 in SRdays) seen (*top*) at Lynton and (*below*) Woody Bay.   *Author's collection*

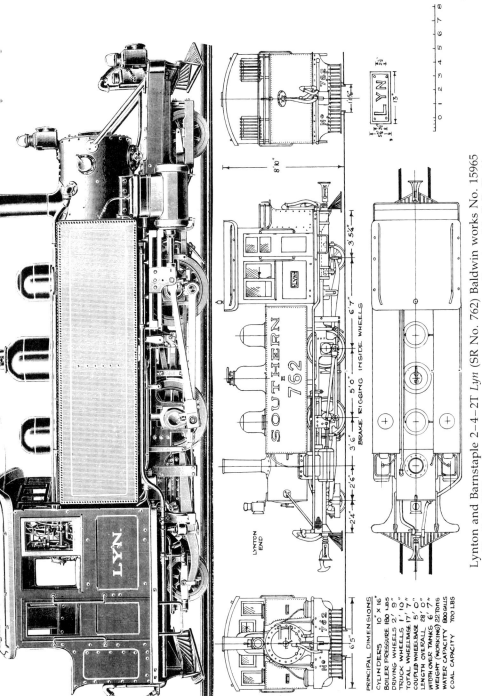

PRINCIPAL DIMENSIONS

CYLINDERS	10" × 16"
BOILER PRESSURE	180 LBS
DRIVING WHEELS	2' 9"
TRUCK WHEELS	1' 10"
TOTAL WHEELBASE	17' 7"
COUPLED WHEELBASE	5' 0"
LENGTH OVERALL	28' 0"
WIDTH OVER TANKS	6' 7"
WEIGHT (WORKING)	22 TONS
WATER CAPACITY	680 GALLS
COAL CAPACITY	700 LBS

Lynton and Barnstaple 2–4–2T *Lyn* (SR No. 762) Baldwin works No. 15965
and built in 1898.

Courtesy Mr R.E. Tustin

The passenger rolling stock consisted of sixteen bogie coaches built by the Bristol Wagon and Carriage Works, and one composite third brake by Shapland & Petter, all being mounted on roller bearings. They were adorned with the company's initials and an ornamental device consisting of a circlet round the arms of the borough of Barnstaple and a deer, the latter representing the type of country through which the line ran. The lower panels were finished in lake, with the upper panels in white, so that the whole effect closely resembled the livery style in use on the LNWR.

The lettering on the waist panels was in gilt block letters, shaded black including "GUARD", "PASSENGER", "SALOON" etc. The roofs were white whilst the lampholders, running gear and underframes were black.

The interiors were furbished in blue cloth (first class) or maroon leather (smoking class). Arm rests were provided, allowing three-a-side in comfort. Third-class passengers, however, had four-a-side wooden seats, described as of the garden seat variety, and slatted with alternate strips of black and white wood. Fixed partitions were fitted between first-class compartments, between firsts and thirds, and to separate smoking and non-smoking thirds. Elsewhere, third-class compartments were divided by sliding partitions, which were bolted to the supporting framework of the luggage racks, or lowered between the seat backs, giving an open interior for the summer.

The principal coach dimensions were as follows:

Length overall	39 ft 6 in.
Length over buffer beams	35 ft 2 in.
Width over bodies	6 ft 0 in.
Width over steps	7 ft 4 in.
Total wheelbase	28 ft 10 in.
Bogie wheelbase	4 ft 4 in.
Wheel diameter	1 ft 6 in.
Height, rail to centre of roof	8 ft 7 in.
Height, solebar to cant rail	6 ft 4½ in.
Height, maximum internal	6 ft 6 in
Weight	8½ to 9 tons (according to type)

The third class coaches (of which returns show ten) had seven compartments; there was one coach comprising one third class compartment, two firsts, a first-class saloon and a first-class open observation end. There were also four coaches with luggage and guards compartment, and one passenger brake van. Composite brake No. 2 comprised a guard's compartment with ducket, a two-door luggage compartment, one third class compartment, a first-class saloon and a first-class observation compartment, in this case having three windows overlooking the track, whereas the observation compartment of the coach mentioned above had a blank end with no windows.

The first goods stock ordered in August 1897 consisted of 14 four wheeled and four bogie vehicles, painted in light grey with white lettering and black ironwork and running gear. The Southern Railway later repainted most wagons in their standard umber livery, white lettering and black running gear. Most vehicles were vacuum fitted and standard centre buffer-couplers. The list on the next page is from official documents.

Several service vehicles were used on the railway and were numbered 441S, 442S & 441SM. The breakdown cranes (Nos. 441S and 442S) were brought into use in 1927 being built by Chambers, Scott & Co., and purchased by the Southern from Messrs George Cohen & Sons. Fitted with outrigger stabilisers they were designed to lift three tons at 15 ft radius. There was little need for a breakdown crane on the Lynton and Barnstaple, where mishaps could normally be tackled with the aid of a couple of jacks, and in consequence one of the cranes, together with the match truck (441SM) spent its life on the long headshunt in Pilton yard. The other was put to use in Lynton goods yard, where it stood on its own length of track ready to lift any heavy load carried by the railway.

Before leaving the subject of locomotives and rolling stock, a note on the valve gear fitted to the Manning, Wardle engines, variously described as modified Joy and modified Walschaert, may be of interest; it is taken from "Model Locomotive Valve Gears" by *Martin Evans*:

> The Joy gear was extensively used in this country at one time, especially by the London and North Western Railway. It was mainly adopted for inside cylinder locomotives, but has also been used for outside cylinders. A good example of the latter application was the gear fitted to the narrow-gauge engines of the old Lynton and Barnstaple Railway.
>
> The Joy valve gear must be regarded as inferior to the Walschaerts' when used outside the locomotive . . . On the other hand, the Joy motion may have an advantage on certain narrow-gauge type locomotives when the driving-wheels are very small, and the motion comes down very low and close to track level.

It certainly can be said that the latter conditions were obtained on the Lynton and Barnstaple locomotives, thus accounting for the selection of the Joy gear.

The permanent way was good, being laid with 40 lb. rails; but it had not the solidity of the Welsh prototype, which employed a chaired road, and the sharper curves of the Lynton line were not easily traversed by the six-coupled engines, so that the track required

Lynton and Barnstaple Railway

Wagons

Number				Date	Body Dimensions			Tare		Capacity	No. of	Original Cost
SR	Old	Class	Builders	Built	Length	Width	Height	T.	Cwts	(Tons)	Wheels	£
28301	12	Open Goods	Bristol C&W Co.	1898	25′ 10¾″	5′ 6½″	4′ 6½″	5	5	8	8	90
28302	13	″	″	1898	25′ 10¾″	5′ 6½″	4′ 6½″	5	5	8	8	90
28303	24	″	″	1913	26′ 1″	5′ 7″	4′ 5¾″	6	–	8	8	90
28304	1	″	″	1898	10′ 0″	5′ 8½″	4′ 9″	2	16	4	4	40
28305	2	″	″	1898	10′ 0″	5′ 8½″	4′ 9″	2	16	4	4	40
28306	8	″	″	1898	10′ 0″	5′ 8½″	4′ 9″	2	16	4	4	40
28307	9	″	″	1898	10′ 0″	5′ 8½″	4′ 9″	2	16	4	4	40
28308	10	″	″	1898	10′ 0″	5′ 8½″	4′ 9″	2	16	4	4	40
28309	11	″	″	1898	10′ 0″	5′ 8½″	4′ 9″	2	16	4	4	40
28310	17	″	″	1898	10′ 0″	5′ 8½″	4′ 9″	2	16	4	4	40
28311	18	″	″	1898	10′ 0″	5′ 8½″	4′ 9″	2	16	4	4	40
28312	19	″	″	1900	20′ 7″	5′ 0½″	4′ 3¼″	3	18	6	8	90
28313	22	″	″	1903	24′ 7″	6′ 3½″	4′ 7″	5	5	8	8	90
28314	20	Platform Truck	″	1902	24′ 7″	6′ 3½″	–	4	–	8	8	90
28315	21	″	Bristol C&W Co.	1902	24′ 7″	6′ 3½″	–	4	–	8	8	90
28316	–	Open Goods	J.F. Howard Bedford	1927	26′ 3½″	6′ 5¾″	4′ 9½″	6	1	8	8	199
28317	–	″	″	1927	26′ 3½″	6′ 5¾″	4′ 9½″	6	1	8	8	199
28318	–	″	″	1927	26′ 3½″	6′ 5¾″	4′ 9½″	6	1	8	8	199
28319	–	″	″	1927	26′ 3½″	6′ 5¾″	4′ 9½″	6	1	8	8	199
47036	3	Covered Goods	Bristol C&W Co.	1898	10′ 5″	5′ 4″	7′ 2½″	2	12	4	4	50
47037	4	″	″	1898	10′ 5″	5′ 4″	7′ 2½″	2	12	4	4	50
47038	6	″	″	1898	10′ 5″	5′ 4″	7′ 2½″	2	12	4	4	50
47039	7	″	″	1898	10′ 5″	5′ 4″	7′ 2½″	2	12	4	4	50
47040	15	″	″	1898	10′ 5″	5′ 4″	7′ 2½″	2	12	4	4	50
47041	16	″	″	1898	10′ 5″	5′ 4″	7′ 2½″	2	12	4	4	50
47042	–	″	J.F. Howard Bedford	1927	26′ 5½″	6′ 10¾″	8′ 6½″	6	12	8	8	232
47043	–	″	″	1927	26′ 5½″	6′ 10¾″	8′ 6½″	6	12	8	8	232
47044	–	″	″	1927	26′ 5½″	6′ 10¾″	8′ 6½″	6	12	8	8	232
47045	–	″	″	1927	26′ 5½″	6′ 10¾″	8′ 6½″	6	12	8	8	232
56039	5	Goods Bke Van	Bristol C&W Co.	1898	24′ 5¾″	6′ 9″	10′ 6½″	5	18	8	8	100
56040	14	″	″	1898	24′ 5¾″	6′ 9″	10′ 6½″	5	18	8	8	100
56041	23	″	″	1908	24′ 6¾″	5′ 10½″	10′ 6½″	5	18	8	8	100

Service Vehicles

Number				Date	Body Dimensions			Tare		Capacity	No. of	Original Cost
441 S	–	Travelling Crane	Purchased second-hand. G. Cohen & Sons	1926								135*
441 SM	–	Match Truck	SRly. Lancing	1927	11′ 3″	6′ 8½″	6′ 6″				8	200
442 S	–	Travelling Crane	Purchased second-hand. G Cohen & Sons	1926								135†

Remarks

* Lifting Capacity 15′ Radius   3 Tons
Lifting Capacity 11′ 6″ Radius   4½ Tons

† Lifting Capacity 15′ Radius   3 Tons
Lifting Capacity 11′ 6″ Radius   4½ Tons

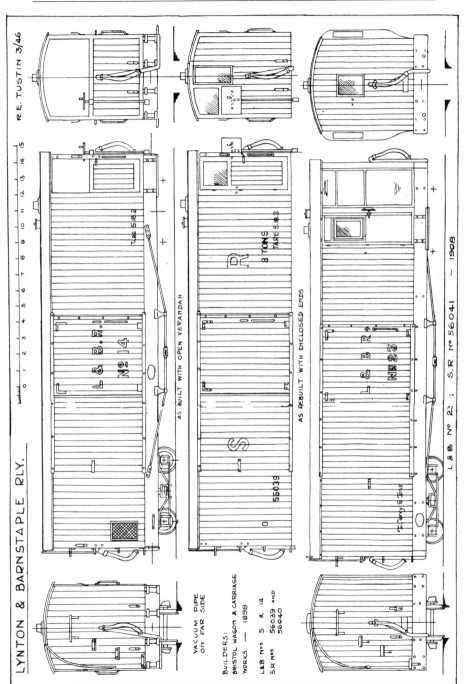

LYNTON & BARNSTAPLE RLY.

R.E. TUSTIN 3/46

L & B R? N? 14

TARE 5.18.2

AS BUILT WITH OPEN VERANDAH

8 TONS

TARE 5.18.2

56039

S

AS REBUILT WITH ENCLOSED ENDS

L & B R? N? 23

To carry 8 tons

L & B N? 23 ; S.R. N? 56041 — 1908

VACUUM PIPE
ON FAR SIDE

BUILDERS:
BRISTOL WAGON & CARRIAGE
WORKS — 1898

L&B N?S 5 & 14
S.R. N?S 56039 AND
56040

Drawings courtesy Mr. R.E. Tustin

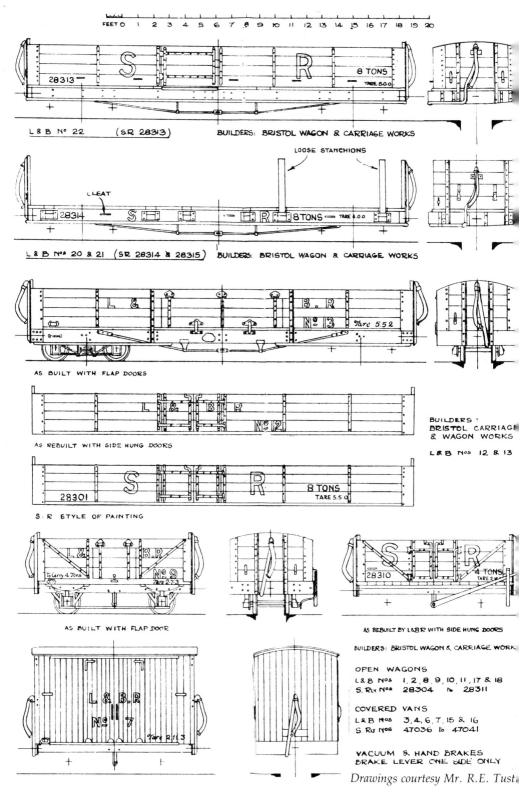

FEET 0 1 2 3 4 5 6 7 8 9 10 11 12 13 14 15 16 17 18 19 20

28313 S R 8 TONS TARE 5.0.0

L & B Nº 22 (S.R. 28313) BUILDERS: BRISTOL WAGON & CARRIAGE WORKS

LOOSE STANCHIONS

CLEAT

28314 S R 8 TONS TARE 4.0.0

L & B Nºs 20 & 21 (SR 28314 & 28315) BUILDERS: BRISTOL WAGON & CARRIAGE WORKS

L & B. R Nº 13 Tare 5.52

AS BUILT WITH FLAP DOORS

L & B R Nº 12

AS REBUILT WITH SIDE HUNG DOORS

BUILDERS:
BRISTOL CARRIAGE
& WAGON WORKS

L & B Nos 12 & 13

28301 S R 8 TONS TARE 5.5 0

S.R. STYLE OF PAINTING

L & B.R Nº 9
To Carry 4 Tons Tare 2.7.3

AS BUILT WITH FLAP DOOR

S R 28310 4 TONS TARE 2..

AS REBUILT BY L&B.R WITH SIDE HUNG DOORS

BUILDERS: BRISTOL WAGON & CARRIAGE WORK

OPEN WAGONS
L & B Nos 1, 2, 8, 9, 10, 11, 17 & 18
S. Ry Nos 28304 to 28311

COVERED VANS
L & B Nos 3, 4, 6, 7, 15 & 16
S. Ry Nos 47036 to 47041

VACUUM & HAND BRAKES
BRAKE LEVER ONE SIDE ONLY

L & B.R Nº 7 Tare 2.11.3

Drawings courtesy Mr. R.E. Tust

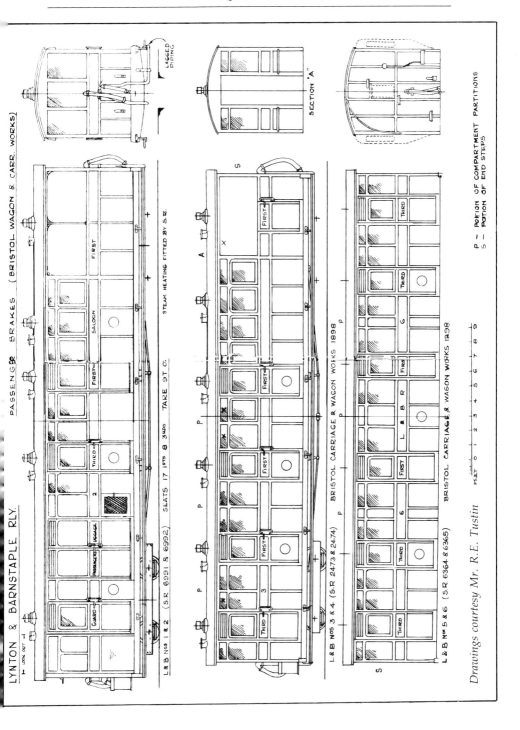

LYNTON & BARNSTAPLE RLY.

PASSENGER BRAKES (BRISTOL WAGON & CARR. WORKS)

SECTION "A"

L&B Nos 1 & 2 (S.R. 6991 & 6992) SEATS 17 1sts 8 3rds TARE 9T 0C.

STEAM HEATING FITTED BY S.R.

L&B Nos 3 & 4 (S.R. 2473 & 2474) BRISTOL CARRIAGE & WAGON WORKS 1898

L&B Nos 5 & 6 (S.R. 6364 & 6365) BRISTOL CARRIAGE & WAGON WORKS 1898

P — PORTION OF COMPARTMENT PARTITIONS
S — PORTION OF END STEPS

FEET 0 1 2 3 4 5 6 7 8 9

Drawings courtesy Mr. R.E. Tustin

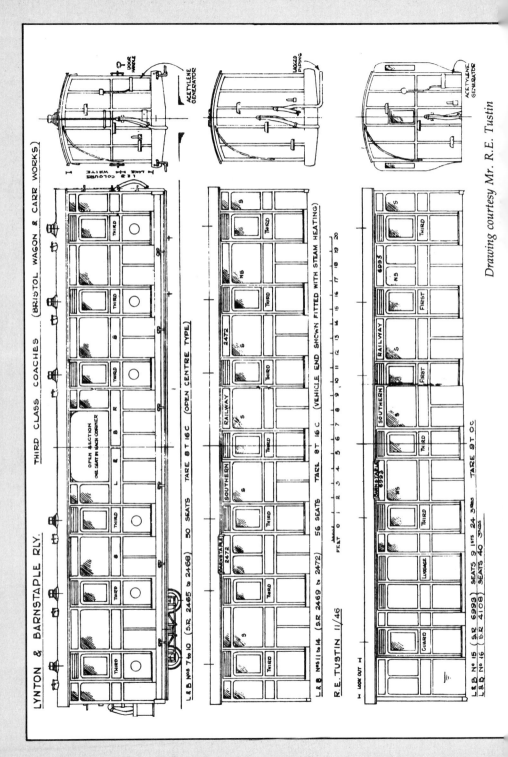

Drawing courtesy Mr. R.E. Tustin

A third class passenger coach No. 9, one of four vehicles with an open compartment in the centre, seen with the altered livery of "LB&R" on the waist band but no circle motif. *LGRP, courtesy David & Charles*

Another style of "open" vehicle, this one No. 2 (in original livery) being a 1st/3rd saloon brake with canvas blinds and a dog box.
Real Photos, courtesy Ian Allan

A busy scene at Lynton with a four coach train awaiting departure to Barnstaple whilst the locomotive picks up the freight traffic from the main platform. *Author's collection*

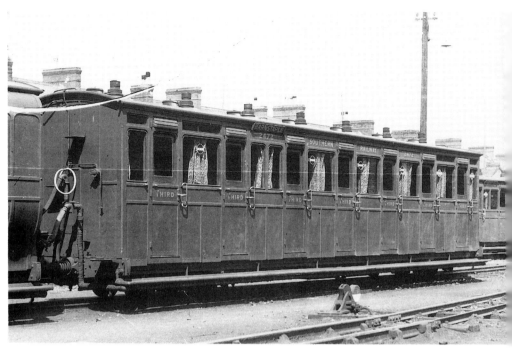

Passenger coach No. 2472 (old No. 14), a third class 56 seat vehicle built by Bristol Carriage & Wagon Co. in 1898, seen here in SR livery and showing the destination board above the coach number.   *LGRP, courtesy David & Charles*

Freight vehicle No. 56040 (formerly No. 14, L&BR), one of the 8-ton bogie brake vans seen here in SR livery at Pilton.   *Author's collection*

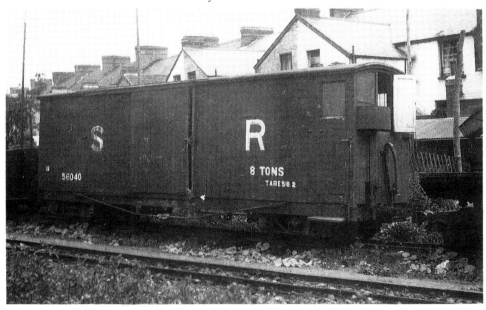

Goods Brake Van No. 23 as delivered by the makers in 1908. Note the "Passenger type" guards ducket and door. *Courtesy Mr R.E. Tustin*

Two views showing a good selection of freight vehicles. The upper photograph shows the box van in both SR livery, with the old L&BR livery showing also. *LGRP, courtesy David & Charles*

Three views of the 4-ton open wagons which used the same chassis design as the box vans. These were mainly used for the transportation of coal. It is interesting to note that the wagon sides are resting on the floor of the vehicle, which can clearly be seen in the top photo of No. 9. The middle photograph is of No. 9 (as new) photographed by the Bristol Wagon and Carriage works. The lower photograph is No. 10 in Pilton Yard. *Author's collection*

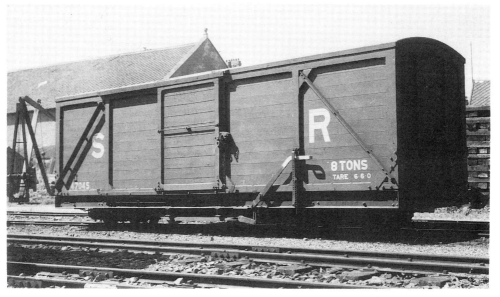

An 8-ton, 8 wheeled bogie van No. 47045 built by J. & F. Howard in 1927 seen here in its SR livery (never painted in L&BR livery) at Pilton Yard.

Author's collection

A scene at the LSWR/L&B trans-shipment siding, with the new 8-ton, 8-wheeled covered goods wagons being delivered, in 1927. One is still on the standard gauge wagon.

Photomatic Ltd

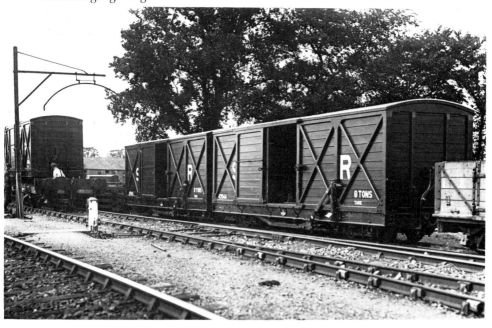

Two Bristol Wagon and Carriage Co. official pictures of No. 13 8-ton, 8 wheeled bogie open goods wagon of 1897 (later SR No. 28302) and No. 14, an 8-ton 8 wheel bogie Brake Van of 1897 (later SR No. 56040).   *Author's collection*

A fine view across Pilton Yard with freight and passenger stock filling all and marked with Lot Numbers for the "great sale" day. *Author's collection*

The two travelling cranes No. 441 and No. 442 built by Chambers Scott and Co. seen here with the Match Truck No. 441SM on sale day. The Lot Nos. were 65, 66 and 67. *Author's collection*

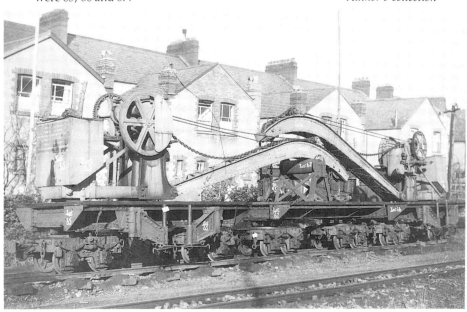

The 1927 8-wheeled open goods bogie wagon on the turntable at Pilton Yard.
Photomatic Collection

A good selection of freight stock on the goods yard road at Pilton depot. The stock is new and sleepers are piled high, being loaded by the yard crane from the pile on the right.
Author's collection

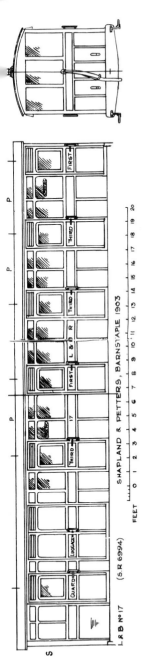

Lynton and Barnstaple Railway

Coaches

Number SR	Old	Class	Builders	Date Built	Height	Width	Length	Weight T.	Cwts	Seats 1st	Seats 3rd	No. of Wheels	Original Cost £
2465	7	Third	Bristol C&W Co.	1898	8'7"	6'0"	35'2"	8	16	–	50	8	560
2466	8	"	"	1898	8'7"	6'0"	35'2"	8	16	–	50	8	560
2467	9	"	"	1898	8'7"	6'0"	35'2"	8	16	–	50	8	560
2468	10	"	"	1898	8'7"	6'0"	35'2"	8	16	–	50	8	560
2469	11	"	"	1898	8'7"	6'0"	35'2"	8	16	–	56	8	600
2470	12	"	"	1898	8'7"	6'0"	35'2"	8	16	–	56	8	600
2471	13	"	"	1898	8'7"	6'0"	35'2"	8	16	–	56	8	600
2472	14	"	"	1898	8'7"	6'0"	35'2"	8	16	–	56	8	600
2473	3	"	"	1898	8'7"	6'0"	35'2"	8	16	–	46	8	800*
2474	4	Third Brake	"	1898	8'7"	6'0"	35'2"	8	16	–	46	8	800*
4108	16	"	"	1898	8'7"	6'0"	35'2"	9	–	–	40	8	800
6364	5	Composite	"	1898	8'7"	6'0"	35'2"	8	16	12	32	8	800
6365	6	"	"	1898	8'7"	6'0"	35'2"	8	16	12	32	8	800
6991	1	Compo. Brake	Bristol C&W Co.	1898	8'7"	6'0"	35'2"	9	–	17	8	8	800
6992	2	"	"	1898	8'7"	6'0"	35'2"	9	–	17	8	8	800
6993	15	"	"	1898	8'7"	6'0"	35'2"	9	–	9	20	8	800†
6994	17	"	Shepherd & Peters Barnstaple	1903	8'7"	6'0"	36'1½"	9	–	9	24	8	600

* Transferred from Composite. 5/25.

† Altered from 24 to 20 Third Class Seats. 4/27.

more care to maintain it in good condition; even so, the trains rolled excessively.

The equipment at the stations was as follows (see Appendix Two for full details):

Barnstaple Town	Run-round loop, transfer siding, and signal cabin.
Snapper Halt	Shelter only.
Chelfham	Passing loop, siding, water tank, and ground frame.
Bretton Fleming	As at Chelfham until 1932 when the passing loop and signal were removed, making Chelfham–Blackmoor one section.
Blackmoor	Passing loop, large goods yard, water tank, and ground frame.
Parracombe Halt	Shelter and water tank.
Woody Bay	As at Blackmoor.
Caffyns Halt	Shelter only.
Lynton	Run-round loop, bay road, engine shed, water column, large goods yard, and ground frame.

The Lynton station buildings were of the same Nuremburg style as those at Woody Bay and Blackmoor, erected by the company; those at Chelfham and Bratton Fleming were built by the contractors Messrs Nuttall & Co. The platforms at all stations were only one brick deep; at Chelfham and Bratton Fleming they were intersected by sidings.

Alterations to the layout at Lynton were made shortly after the opening of the line. Double slips at the up end of the station were replaced by a pair of points, the crossover at the down end was reversed, and a new siding laid in, avoiding the goods shed and extending the length of the goods yard. The home signal was replaced by a bracket signal to admit trains to the bay road.

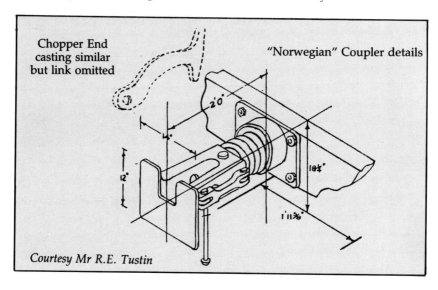

Chopper End casting similar but link omitted

"Norwegian" Coupler details

Courtesy Mr R.E. Tustin

Chapter Four
The Route Described

To become more fully acquainted with the characteristics of the railway we should do well to imagine ourselves on a trip from Barnstaple to Lynton. The length of platform face at Barnstaple Town available for Lynton line trains is 320 feet. When the station was built, space was reserved for an arrival platform adjacent to North Walk, but it was not constructed. The proposal, however, accounts for the very long-lead point at the end of the run-round loop, for the latter was laid out as a running road.

Leaving the Town station the line follows the curve of North Walk and crosses the Braunton Road upon the level, passing on the left the old quay siding that was used extensively at one time for receiving building materials consigned to Lynton. Beyond the second level crossing (Pilton Road) we run through Pilton yard, the "base" of the company, accommodating locomotive and carriage sheds, repair shops, the manager's offices and an extensive goods yard. The running line here forms a passing loop, but no passing was ever (so far as is known) carried out here. Escaping from suburban Barnstaple, we enter the pleasant valley of the Yeo. (Hereabouts the engines of Up trains commence their shrill and prolonged whistling, a signal to the gatemen at Pilton Road and Braunton Road.) We cross a mill leat and the river four times before striking a short incline – half a mile at 1 in 55. The gradient eases to 1 in 528 for the following 1½ miles, in which we pass Snapper Halt (for Goodleigh) adjacent to the main road; next we must take particular note of the second bridge over the Yeo – Collar Bridge – for it marks the foot of the 1 in 50 grade that continues almost without break for eight miles. Although the valley is wide, the line follows a winding course, and we ricochet from side to side without apparent reason; the opposition of landowners did not allow the engineer freedom in the choice of the route.

Rounding an extremely long curve and changing our direction from north to east, we burrow under the main road and ascend from the floor of the valley to gain a hill-side location that remains typical for the remainder of the journey. Increasingly extensive views are obtained from the left-hand windows, with Chelfham viaduct prominent ahead. The exhaust of our locomotive becomes more audible to us as we climb through the woods (especially if *Lyn* is in charge) and, echoing from the hills, heralds our approach to Chelfham (locally pronounced "Chilham"). Chelfham viaduct has eight spans, each 42 ft wide, rises to about 70 ft above the Stoke Rivers valley, and is the principal engineering structure upon the railway. More than a quarter of a million bricks were used in its construction, and the cost was about £6,500. The station, immediately beyond the viaduct, is charmingly situated in a wood (one of many planted by the company

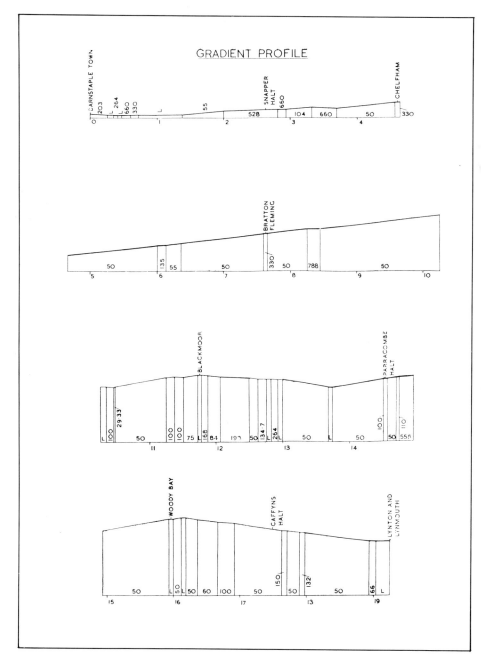

The Gradient Profile of the line.

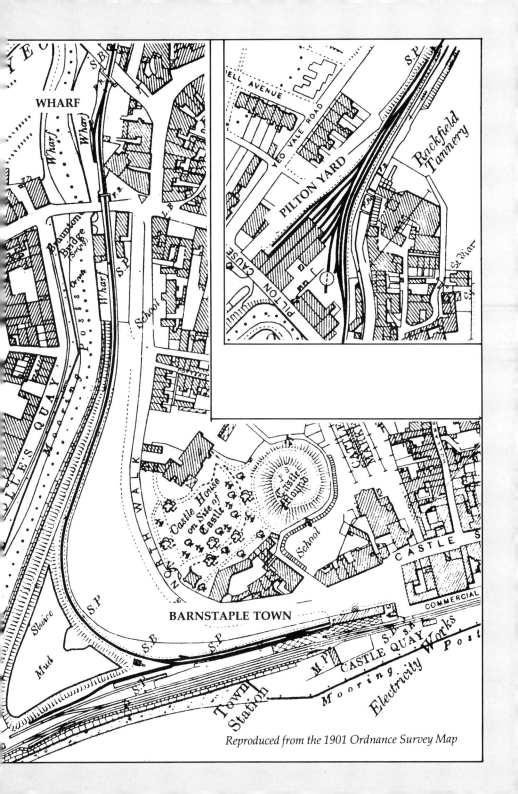

WHARF

PILTON YARD

Rackfield Tannery

BARNSTAPLE TOWN

Castle House on Site of Castle

Castle House

Town Station

CASTLE QUAY

Electricity Works

Reproduced from the 1901 Ordnance Survey Map

SNAPPER HALT

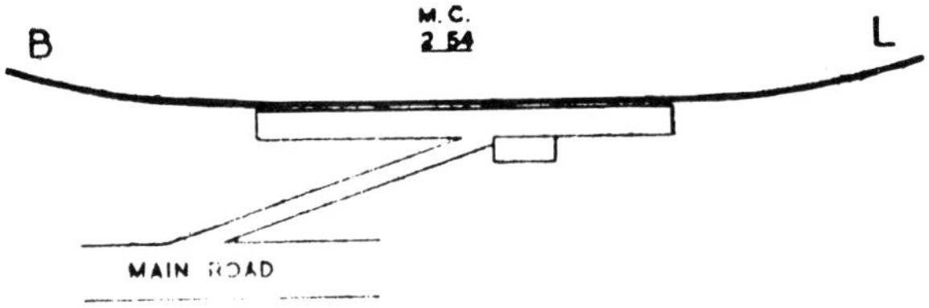

M.C.
2 54

B   L

MAIN ROAD

CHELFHAM

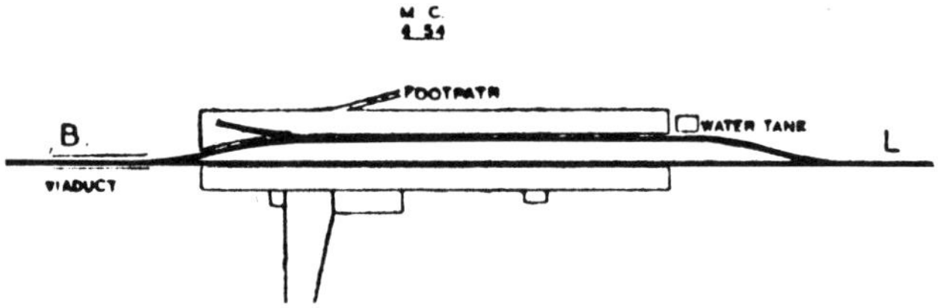

M C
4 54

FOOTPATH

B   WATER TANK   L

VIADUCT

BRATTON FLEMING

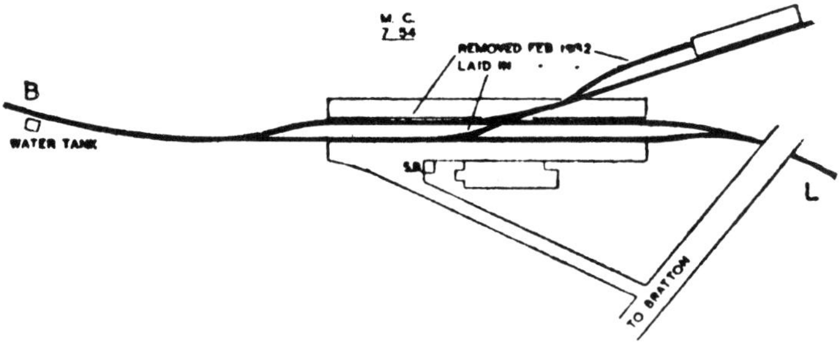

M.C.
7 54

REMOVED FEB 1932
LAID IN

B

WATER TANK

S.B.

TO BRATTON

L

BLACKMOOR

M.C.
11 62

B   REMOVED SEPT 1930

WATER TANK

MAIN

L

EXTENDED
SEPT 1930

S.B.

STABLES

ROAD

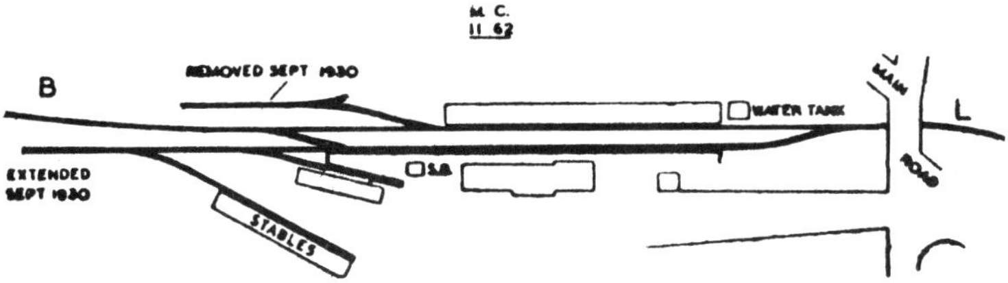

PARRACOMBE HALT

M.C.
14 33

B   WATER
TANK   L

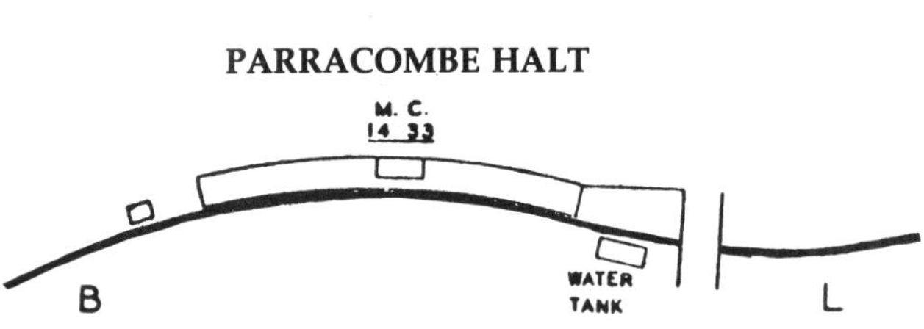

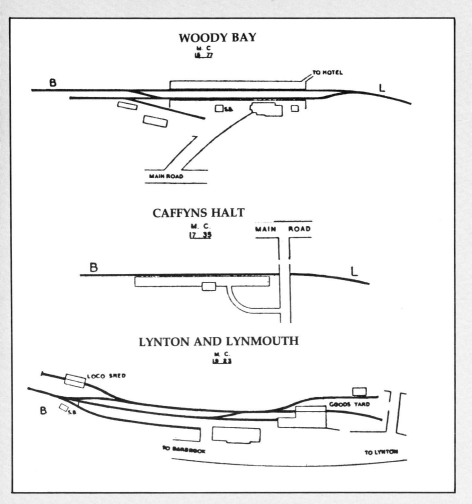

WOODY BAY
M. C.
18 77

B · · · L

TO HOTEL

S.B.

MAIN ROAD

CAFFYNS HALT
M. C.
17 39

MAIN ROAD

B · · · L

LYNTON AND LYNMOUTH
M. C.
18 23

LOCO SHED

B

S.B.

GOODS YARD

TO BARBROOK

TO LYNTON

in an attempt to conceal the scars caused by construction) and is named after a large farmstead half a mile away on the right. It serves the villages of Stoke Rivers (1½ miles), Shirwell (2¼ miles), and Loxhore (1¾ miles).

Whilst the engine is taking water we shall have time to admire the view from the end of the platform, noting that the line has again turned northwards before springing across the valley. On our right is Youlston Wood, at one time a favourite haunt of wild deer, and we should notice also Northleigh hill, standing high above the viaduct, for a stranger might be surprised to learn that our locomotive will haul us to not only an equal height but half as high again within the next eight miles. It was at this station that a driver, many years ago, once mislaid his train. The engine of an Up train, having carried out some shunting, proceeded light to Barnstaple, the driver being ignorant that the passengers in his discarded coaches were showing impatience at the long delay. On arrival at Pilton Yard, however, he was asked what he had done with his train. Having no satisfactory explanation to offer, he had the humiliating duty of returning to Chelfham, where, presumably, a suitable reception awaited him.

Leaving Chelfham we discern the River Yeo continuing its course northwards while we climb steadily in a more easterly direction a hundred feet or so above an unchristened stream. Vast expenditure would have been avoided if the line had followed the less rugged valley of the Yeo. One might safely say that the fortunes of the railway would have been less blighted if it had been able to reach Blackmoor *via* Kentisbury and Little Ley (for Combe Martin); but we are left to assume that landowners' oppositon again decided the matter. After a deep rock cutting we pass beneath the main road; then follows a succession of reverse curves past Chumhill. If we are seated in the fourth coach (the maximum number allowed for one engine) we shall obtain frequent views, without having to put our heads out of the window, of our steed nosing its way round the curves. Lancey Brook viaduct is now crossed, approached by curved embankments. It is 28 feet high and has eight spans. A less tortuous course now brings us to Bratton Fleming, and we notice, before entering the station, an old quarry on the right-hand side of the line which was used to supply ballast to the track, and a water tank with a hand-operated pump beneath. From the platforms, extensive views are obtained of the wooded valley, but it is probably the situation of the station itself, high up on the hill-side and embowered in roses, that appeals most to the average passenger. The station serves not only the large village of Bratton Fleming (½ mile) but, according to a finger-post at the station approach, the more distant hamlets of Challacombe and High Bray (4½ miles).

Two fine views of Barnstaple Station taken in June 1925 showing (*top*) the buffer stops of the Lynton and Barnstaple Railway and (*lower*) the almost 90° curve to the right of the Lynton and Barnstaple Railway, past the signalbox and trans-shipment siding. Note wagon No. 10 very heavily loaded with coal.   *Author's collection*

A view from the trans-shipment siding towards the buffers of Barnstaple station showing the station nameboard and L & BR water column.

LGRP, courtesy David & Charles

A view looking the other way from the station platform showing the main LSWR line on the extreme left, the trans-shipment sidings (*middle left*), the signalbox and the "mainline" of the Lynton and Barnstaple Railway going around to the right on to Pilton Yard. *LGRP, courtesy David & Charles*

Barnstaple signalbox with the trans-shipment siding behind and the main line running in front.

Author's collection

A passenger train just out of Barnstaple Town passing Rolle Quay with the masts of the sail boats clearly visible. The mill on the right was owned by Stanbury and Sons and had a standard gauge siding from the LSWR main line. *Author's collection*

A good view of Pilton Yard in 1936 but this time from the shed door clearly showing the main line (*on the right*) and the goods yard coach stock and engine roads all merging into the main line in the distance. *R.W. Kidner*

Snapper Halt was the first stopping place out of Barnstaple Town and had a small waiting shelter on its short platform. This mainly served the village of Goodleigh.   *Lens of Sutton*

An early view of Chelfham viaduct which stood 70 ft high over the Stoke Rivers Valley.   *Author's collection*

A train arrives at Chelfham station from Barnstaple seen here just coming off the viaduct. Note the stationmaster with the single line token ready to hand to the engine crew and the permanent way trolley on the other line.
Author's collection

Just easing-up is this Barnstaple train for Lynton, seen here crossing the Chelfham viaduct. *Author's collection*

A fine view of the trackwork and point rodding at the Barnstaple end of Chelfham Station. *Lens of Sutton*

Two views of Chelfham station both showing the idyllic setting for the line. The bottom view portrays the simple stone structure and tiled roof with the small signal cabin on the left. Note the luggage barrow, post box, Nestlé chocolate machine, seat and above all the Great Northern poster for Skegness!

LGRP, courtesy David & Charles

The station of Bratton Fleming (initially only Bratton) with just the single line in place, towards the end of its life. The signal cabin is just visible to the right of the white porch.

Author's collection

A view of Bratton in the very early days showing the additional nameboard of "Fleming" placed underneath Bratton, looking towards Barnstaple. *Author's collection*

Below. A fine old official postcard view of Bratton showing the station buildings, signal cabin, the line to the left to the shed and tall signal on the approach to the station. Note the travelling baskets, one being marked PERKINS B'HAM. *Author's collection*

Blackmoor station with its chalet-style buildings and a water tower at the
Lynton end of the station and with a normal Lynton and Barnstaple water
column to the Barnstaple end. The track layout consisted of a good length
passing loop with a long head shunt on the "up" line with access to two
sidings. These serviced a goods shed and stables. A small siding was provided on the down side and the top photograph shows a spare coach
standing on the line.   *Author's collection*

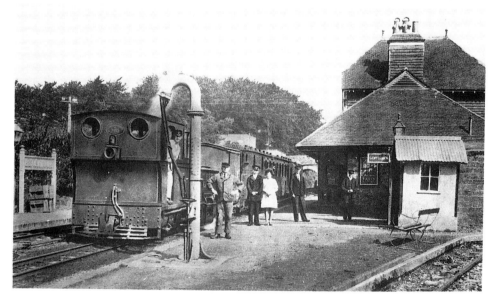

Parracombe Halt, a simple wooden shelter on a 213 ft long, rail level platform. Ironically the village of Parracombe was one of the more substantial on the line yet the station modest indeed.   *Lens of Sutton*

Parracombe Halt in later days with the "new" SR concrete shelter structure as used on their standard gauge lines. The village church can clearly be seen as also the post box on the side of the shelter.   *Author's collection*

A fine view in 1935 from the road bridge looking down on Parracombe Halt with the train using the water tank situated near the bridge.   *R.W. Kidner*

An early postcard of Wooda Bay station (later Woody Bay). A fine collection of enamel signs can be seen.   *Lens of Sutton*

This view of Woody Bay station shows the down platform devoid of any shelter and the chalet style station buildings on the up platform. A head shunt on the up line gave access to a single siding. The locomotive *Yeo* is about to start for Lynton, with the station staff about to hand over the token, in May 1935.   *Author's collection*

Looking towards Lynton with the two SR rail built signals and the old Lynton and Barnstaple Railway Evans O'Donnell wooden signal still in place and a Barnstaple train signalled.   *LGRP, courtesy David & Charles*

Caffyns Halt looking towards Lynton. This simple Halt served a golf course and so trains basically stopped only on request.

LGRP, courtesy David & Charles

Looking towards Barnstaple with the station nameboard stating (for Golf Links) and also in this view, a station light has been provided on the rather unstable looking shelter.

R.W. Kidner

Lynton Station, the terminus of the Lynton & Barnstaple Railway. Here is seen the substantial station buildings and goods shed. In the early track layout, a double slip was situated at the station throat giving access to the bay platform but this was removed and replaced by simple turnouts.

Lens of Sutton

A fine view of the station layout taken from the up signal post in 1935. This shows the SR improvements of the bracket starter signal and ground frame hut (in the bushes). The construction of a station master's bungalow can also be seen. *R.W. Kidner*

The permanent way gang stand back so that the train can leave. Note the nameboard style. *Author's collection*

An official postcard of Lynton station showing the immaculate turnout of the Lynton and Barnstaple Railway. Note all the carriage doors are open, the new open wagons, the smart station staff and the fireman up on the locomotive preparing for the run to Barnstaple. *Author's collection*

The goods shed showing the construction and attractive stonework.
LGRP, courtesy David & Charles

The station buildings at Lynton in SR days showing the slate-hung facings on the upper storey as a protection from the prevailing weather.
LGRP, courtesy David & Charles

Another fine Victorian view of Lynton station with locomotive *Taw* in full steam ready for its run to Barnstaple. Note the access to the motion and valves open for servicing and oiling. The livery lining also can be seen well on the locomotive.   *Author's collection*

The substantial single-road engine shed at Lynton, being built of stone and roofed in corrugated iron. Entrance was originally from the far end but the track layout was revised to form a run round loop. Note the battening on the outer walls placed there presumably to allow enamel signs to be hung for advertising.   *Lens of Sutton*

Continuing from Bratton the line encircles two side valleys on embankments 40 feet high, the gradient easing on them to 1 in 788. Almost immediately, however, the gradient returns to its former severity. We thread a winding path along the steep hill-side past several picturesque farms – Knightacott, Narracott, Sprecott and Hunnacott – and at more than one point a stream is led above us through a concrete aqueduct. Deep rock cuttings and high embankments are passed in rapid succession, and the difficulties which beset the engineer in constructing this part of the line are apparent. The necessity of avoiding farm buildings and cottages where there is no latitude on the steep hill-side and the negotiation, with curves of not less than 5 chains radius, of numerous side valleys combined to prevent the maintenance of the nominal ruling gradient of 1 in 50. The climb, therefore, is interrupted by a short length of level, followed by a descent at 1 in 100 and a sudden, though extremely short, ascent at 1 in 30, which fortunately can be easily "rushed". The nature of the line is now decidedly reminiscent of the Festiniog Railway, the formation being supported by long retaining walls, and the railway continues to twist and turn, as though attempting to keep a high position above the tumbling stream; but, finding it impossible, it sweeps round half a circle and escapes from the valley through a cutting below Wistlandpound Farm. The gradient eases to Blackmoor station, where a welcome respite is granted to our hard-pressed locomotive. The buildings here were planned on an extensive scale, for this was intended to be the principal intermediate station, serving a number of villages, and to accommodate the horses and coaches of a connecting road service to Ilfracombe. For many years after the opening of the line refreshment rooms were maintained here and at Lynton.

The gradient now falls for two miles, gradually at first, then more steeply at 1 in 50 as far as a very large curved embankment spanning the valley of the River Heddon at Parracombe. After a view of the distant hills known as Great and Little Hangman and of the four sides of Parracombe Church, we pull up at Parracombe halt, where there is a good supply of water for our locomotive. Climbing again for another mile and a half we arrive at the summit point of the railway, Woody Bay station ("Wooda Bay" until 1901), 980 feet above sea-level and 16 miles from Barnstaple, amidst moorland scenery where trees are scarce but rabbits plentiful. During our climb, almost from sea-level, we have passed through three distinct types of scenery – first, the pastures of the Yeo vale, secondly, the wooded slopes round the foot of Bratton Down, and thirdly the rocky moorland itself, parts of which, however, are under cultivation as arable land. Close to Woody

Bay station is a large hotel of the same name which, we are pleased to learn from an advertisement in an early timetable, possessed the luxury of a bathroom; but otherwise there is little sign of habitation in the neighbourhood, the station having been intended to serve the "rising water-place" two miles distant. Unfortunately for the railway this Peter Pan of resorts failed to rise sufficiently (or even perceptibly), and the optimism displayed by the company's prospectus has remained unjustified. About 1905 Princess Christian and Princess Victoria came to this station in the course of a tour of North Devon beauty spots.

Beyond the station the line runs through a deep rock cutting and resumes its hill-side location on a falling gradient of 1 in 50, but the views are now on the right-hand side, of fascinating valleys that run away up to the purple highlands of Exmoor. A mile and a half from Woody Bay station we call at Caffyns Halt (for the Golf Course) and pass beneath the main road again at Dean Steep, the scene of a landslide in 1903. The road now descends rapidly to the floor of the valley, while we admire the scenery from a ledge about 150 feet above, and, after a curve at Barbrook, Lynton station is seen on our right but is lost to view as we follow the contour of the hill through a wood, appearing again suddenly when the brakes are applied for the last time and the train pulls up at the picturesque terminus, 250 feet above the town and 700 feet above sea-level.

Lynton & Barnstaple Railway Co.

The Lynton Station Water Supply has failed, and the public are requested to refrain from using the Station lavatories.

By Order.

Chapter Five

The Early Years

From what has been said the difficulties of the company when the line opened for traffic are obvious, and it will be understood that the financial burdens prevented the directors from carrying out those improvements which they knew to be required, among which the extension of the railway at Lynton figured conspicuously. In 1901 a petition was signed by 400 persons requesting the company to act in the matter; but at the following half-yearly meeting the Lynton company's chairman merely suggested that the District Council should construct a good road up to the station as a more practical method of solving the difficulty, pointing out several objections, from the engineering aspect, to the various schemes of extension which had been put up by the petitioners. It was generally known, however, that the real obstacle lay in the difficulty of raising additional capital, for no further attempts on a similar scale were made, and more than twenty years elapsed before a new approach road was built.

The altitude at which the Lynton terminus was situated proved to be a greater disadvantage than had been expected, for the company itself suffered from its elevated postion. During dry summers the station water supply invariably failed at a time when fine weather was encouraging heavy passenger traffic. On these occasions a printed notice was displayed at the station, bearing this request: "LYNTON AND BARNSTAPLE RAILWAY COMPANY. The Lynton station water supply has failed, and the public are requested to refrain from using the station lavatories. By Order." For other than sanitary purposes water was brought by rail from Barnstaple in a large tank mounted on an open wagon. The locomotives, by taking as much water as possible at Parracombe on the down journey, were just able to dispense with the supply at Lynton; shunting or other delays always caused anxiety at these times.

Complaints about the oscillation of carriages continued for many years, and the company announced, in an endeavour to allay the fears of the nervous, that the rolling motion was due to the springs under the carriages being placed transversely instead of longitudinally, adding reassuringly that "not the slightest apprehension of danger need be felt." Nevertheless, the permanent way was strengthened by increasing the number of sleepers to each rail.

The roller bearings with which the carriages were equipped were already giving trouble. Owing to uneven wear the rollers became tapered, and to correct the fault the coaches were turned on the turntable at Pilton Yard. This did not have the desired effect, however, and renewals were made with plain bearings as overhauls became due.

Suggestions that the service could be speeded up were also plentiful, although impracticable, for the time spent at intermediate stations could not be cut down so long as mixed trains were worked, and higher speeds could not be considered in the interests of safety. An allowance of 100 minutes for a distance of 19¼ miles certainly appeared to be more than ample, but it was not so in practice, when shunting had to be performed at several stations. No blame attached to the gallant little locomotives, which fully justified their makers' confidence. Again, the impossibility of providing a service to satisfy all requirements was said to be due to the railway's necessary dependence upon the service and punctuality of its two large neighbours at Barnstaple. On the whole, bearing in mind the pressing need for economy, a satisfactory compromise was reached.

Among various minor complaints were requests for a shelter to be provided at Parracombe Halt and for a footpath to Chelfham station, which would shorten the journey between it and the village of Loxhore, 1¾ miles away. As the railway passed within a mile of the village the inhabitants would have been served more conveniently by a halt of their own, but apparently they were not so rash as to suggest such a blessing, for the footpath may be seen to-day, close to the down side platform. Sir George Newnes realised the publicity value of well-kept stations, and to encourage the staff to take an interest in platform horticulture he offered an annual prize of £5 to be awarded to the station-master whose station possessed the most attractive flower beds. In August 1899, the first prize went to Mr Mintern of Bratton Fleming, and the second to Mr Garrad at Woody Bay.

Line-side flora were fostered also by the Rev J.F. Chanter, of Parracombe. It was the custom of this gentleman to scatter seed broadcast from the carriage window in the early days of the railway, and the abundance of coloured and "evening" primroses was doubtless due to his considerate action.

The little line settled down to a placid existence – far too placid, in the opinion of many people – relieved only by an occasional landslide or snowstorm. The worst storm that the railway ever experienced occurred in February 1900, when the whole of North Devon was covered with snow, and traffic upon the Lynton line was entirely suspended. An account of this event from the pages of the *Devon and Exeter Gazette* indicates that the storm was exceptionally severe, the graphic description stating that "great interference with the traffic on the Lynton and Barnstaple Railway has been occasioned by snow, the line having been impassable for several days. The deepest cuttings were packed with snow drifts, which in some places were eight or ten feet deep. Tuesday night's mail train from Barnstaple to Lynton could not get further than Woody Bay where she ran out into a deep drift and the engine which was sent out to assist her got blocked on the way between Bratton and Blackmoor. An attempt was made yesterday morning to run the first train from Barnstaple, the 6.22 am, with the morning mails. After great difficulty she cut her way through as far as Chelfham station, 4½ miles from Barnstaple, reaching there about 8.45 am. The passengers who had started for Lynton by Tuesday's 4 o'clock train were taken on to Lynton from Woody Bay by Messrs Jones Bros' four-horse coach, which had been driven to Woody Bay for their relief. No train had arrived at Barnstaple from Lynton up to last night and, therefore, no letters had been received. A gang of about a dozen men is at work clearing the line." The comments of Mr Charles Drewett, then secretary to the L&BR company, explain the problem to be faced. "Our difficulties with snow", he said, "were accentuated by drifts blown into the narrow cuttings, necessitating removal of the snow by trucks and unloading at the nearest open place. The working space in the cuttings was so restricted that only a few men could get to work until some space was cleared. Even if a 'plough' had been available it would have been useless, for the snow would have been compressed into a solid mass in the cuttings, making removal even more difficult."

Dean Steep, near Lynton, was the scene of a considerable landslide in June 1903, when about 50 tons of rock and earth collapsed upon the track and dislocated traffic for a day. Fortunately the 6.35 am down train had passed only a few minutes before, and communication was maintained by working trains from Barnstaple and Lynton to either side of the block, and after exchange of passengers, returning to their starting points.

Engineering renewals were not very numerous during the first few years, and included merely the replacement of a number of small underline bridges and the timbers of Lancey Brook viaduct, near Bratton Fleming; indeed, the construction of the line had been extremely satisfactory. The skill with which the trains were handled was reflected in the fact that derailments were almost unknown, which was indeed fortunate, for the location of the line was quite precipitous at many places.

A prophetic forecast of the Railway's fortunes was uttered in a few lines which appeared in the *Pall Mall Gazette* some three years after the opening of the railway; it shows that the line was constructed contrary to much local opinion – the opinion of those who knew the locality far more thoroughly than the hasty promoters. The strangely foreboding article, entitled "Our Own Little Railway", said:

> When we first began to "move" in Lynton and Lynmouth, about the year when the "Lorna Doone" coach commenced running daily, in summer, between Minehead and Lynton, we were a very primitive people, and our primitiveness, especially as regards our distance of nineteen miles

from the nearest railway station, fascinated our few summer visitors, among whom were artists, literary men, two or three actors, some fishermen and a sprinkling of hunting men, some single, others with families, all forming a sociable community. To them the long drive by coach or carriage over the purple moorland from Minehead, or by the picturesque though less wild route from Barnstaple to Lynton was an inducement rather than the contrary. Our visitors of those days spent money freely for keep of man and beast, and stayed with us for weeks or months at a time. Although visitors, tourists and coaches were gradually multiplying, we smiled, in the 'eighties, at the wild talk of some of our younger men of the possibilites of a railway from Barnstaple to Blackmoor Gate, about eight miles from Lynton.

But, collectively speaking, we were ambitious, and a little ashamed of our simplicity. Our local tradesfolk and hotelkeepers began to make money and go away "for a change" in the winter. They came back from places like Torquay, Bournemouth and Brighton with new clothes and new ideas. In due course the rough Lynmouth beach, with its huge rocks on the west of the old pier and light-tower, which have figured in numberless Royal Academy Exhibitions, was covered with an esplanade. This was soon knocked to pieces by the winter seas, but was subsequently restored on a firmer basis. A "funiculaire" lift railway was then put up, a cruel gash being made on the side of the hill for the purpose, to facilitate transit between Lynmouth at the bottom of the hill and Lynton on the top. Lynmouth village, which many artists maintain is, or at any rate has been, the most picturesque in England, with its thatched roofs and whitewashed walls, its gurgling river, and the valley of the Lyn in the distance, is threatened with transformation into a state of unsightly villa-ny; Lynton, the outward charm of which lay in the irregularity of the house, has now its "street" of small dwellings of stereotyped pattern, and the centuries-old church is almost smothered by an overtowering hotel at its very gate. Then wise men – men who some of us thought wise – came from the East, business and professional men from London, and pitied and patronized us of the West and advised us. Some of them would probably, if they could, have surmounted Castle Rock with a dancing booth, made a race-course of the Valley of Rocks, and put up a gin-palace on the Foreland.

One wiser than the rest – perhaps wiser now than then – said we must have a railway, and the most headstrong among us echoed, "We must." The simplest way to get one was obviously through one of the two companies running into Barnstaple. Each of them, the Great Western and the South Western, was approached in turn, but – by mutual agreement, it is said – they held aloof, preferring to leave the financing of such a venture-some undertaking to amateurs. There was nothing left but, as our wise friends told us, to make the railway ourselves – and our fortunes at the same time. Apart from a splendid dividend – we were told how much – the value of property and trade would rise rapidly. A London barrister, a local resident who had run a sheep farm in Australia, and a local shopkeeper who had lived all his life nineteen miles from a railway, were the moving spirits of the directorate. Money flowed in from all local quarters –

from certain of the hotel proprietors, nearly all the tradesmen, from farmers and working men, several of the latter investing the savings of years in the enterprise. It was a great day of hopefulness and rejoicing when the first sod was turned, and even a greater day when the first train left Lynton for Barnstaple three years ago. A railway all our very own! We were doing what two great railway companies had been afraid to do because they did not know as much about it as we did.

But what a day of realization, of reckoning and humiliation, when the chairman presented the Board's last half-yearly report in the real town hall which is Lynton's latest joy. What a sad story of unforeseen expenditure, inadequate and decreasing passenger traffic, of a dividendless past and immediate future – of cash assets little more than sufficient to repair a locomotive! And the places for which the railway was to do so much have little to show by way of compensation. More people have come into Lynton, but mostly day trippers, who have revolutionised the character of the district . . . We who threw cold water on the railway scheme and other "improvements", and were called "old women" for our pains, rejoice, not because our incautious neighbours have sown in order that the shareholders of another railway may reap – it is more than probable that one of the trunk lines will, at its own price, buy up our very own little railway before long – but that the local epidemic of "improving" has received a timely check.

The moral of this story is two-fold. In hastily striving to make new acquaintances one may lose old friends. Running a railway is an expensive game for amateurs.

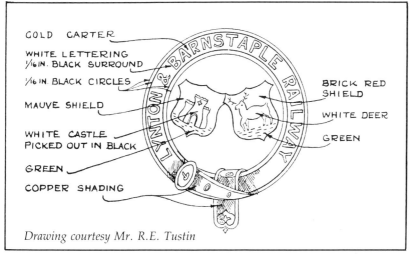

Drawing courtesy Mr. R.E. Tustin

The crest of the Lynton and Barnstaple Railway with a guide to its colours.

LYNTON AND BARNSTAPLE RAILWAY.

(182 A)

MANAGER'S OFFICE,

BARNSTAPLE.

C. E DREWETT, Secretary and Manager.

Our reference

Your reference

To...

....

.... 19

Dear Sir,

LYNTON & BARNSTAPLE RAILWAY.

(89)

From BARNSTAPLE TOWN

To WOODY BAY,

Consignee_____

Out of Foreign Truck No. _____

Contents _____

LYNTON AND BARNSTAPLE RAILWAY.

(99A)

From BARNSTAPLE TOWN

To LYNTON,

Consignee_____

Out of Foreign Truck No. _____

Contents_____

K.D.S. 4019 K.

LYNTON & BARNSTAPLE RAILWAY.

(160)

To STORES DEPARTMENT

(PILTON YARD).

Description ....

_____

Station from ....

FOR REPAIRS.

Chapter Six
Progress

The difficulties faced by the courageous little company were almost insuperable; but under the capable management of Mr Charles E. Drewett, who had succeeded Mr Frank Chanter as secretary and general manager in April 1899, the railway built up a growing popularity with the holiday-maker, though the shortness of the summer season was always a great disadvantage. Mr Drewett had served for many years upon the relief staff of the LSWR, and his father also had early association with that company, having printed the first issue of the *South Western Gazette* and the historical work *A Royal Road* by (Sir) Sam Fay. Mr Drewett's varied experience in railway matters was an inestimable asset in the task of management which he continued to execute efficiently until 1923, when the line became part of the Southern Railway. An enterprise for which he was responsible, and one that carried the name of the company to all parts of the world, was the issue of a remarkable set of coloured post-cards, illustrating various scenes along the railway. They were published in sets of ten under the name of "Peacock", the views having been taken specially by Messrs Major, Darker and Loraine, of Barnstaple. Great care was taken to reproduce the colours of the engines and rolling stock in their correct shades, so that they were among the finest railway postcards ever issued.

The company's failure to capture the Ilfracombe-Lynton traffic was due to many causes which had been overlooked in drawing up the plans. First, the saving of time for the overall journey was so slight as to be of no value at all; secondly, the changes at Blackmoor were unpopular with the public; thirdly, whereas road coaches brought their passengers right into Lynton, the railway deposited them on a hill-side some distance away; and fourthly (a very strong point), the coach drivers, according to ancient custom, were provided with a substantial meal (gratis), at the destination, so that the break of journey and long wait at Blackmoor were extremely unpopular with them. The company also found it inconvenient to reserve sufficient accommodation in the train for the Ilfracombe passengers, whose numbers could not be foretold with accuracy; and so it abandoned the experiment.

But Sir George Newnes was not defeated yet. Being a pioneer automobilist he announced in April 1903 his intention to operate a motor coach service between Ilfracombe and Blackmoor Station *via* Berrydown, thus avoiding Combe Martin hill. This was the first time that a railway company had used road motors on a feeder service, and the two vehicles, passing through Exeter *en route* to Ilfracombe, caused quite a stir in the city. Even this bold stroke was to be a failure, however, for it was found necessary to run at a good pace on the level to make up the time spent on the long hill out of Ilfracombe. The unfortunate sequel to this speeding was thus briefly announced in the local press shortly after the cars had begun operation: "One of these cars was travelling at a little over 8 mph on a bye-road when the police interfered, a prosecution was instituted and a heavy fine inflicted. Sir George Newnes has now decided to stop running the cars over this route." The failure of this short-lived enterprise was another blow to the company, whose chairman evidently regarded the police as being prejudiced against the innovation, for he referred to the matter at a subsequent meeting. "An attempt", he said, "was made during last year to establish motor car communication between Ilfracombe and Blackmoor Gate in order to develop the Ilfracombe and Lynton traffic. The expense was not undertaken by the railway company but by private enterprise which, of course, the company encouraged. The magistrates, however, in their desire, to prevent as far as possible a development of their district, took such steps as to prevent this motor car traffic from being run, and the cars were accordingly sold to the GWR, who, it is to be hoped, would find the authorities more reasonable in the districts where they were to be used." The name of the company founded by Sir George Newnes for the operation of the motor service was the Ilfracombe Motor Company, and it is interesting to recall that the cars were used by the GWR on the Helston–Lizard route where, presumably, the authorities were "more reasonable", but where, in fact, the road is more favourable for fast running.

Although efforts to attract passengers were not always successful, it was some compensation that the freight traffic showed a steady increase, so that additional rolling stock had to be built and the yards at Bratton Fleming and Lynton enlarged. Hopes were raised in 1904 when it was stated that large quantities of slate existed near the line and might be a means of adding to the revenue of the company. On examination, however, it was found to be of such poor quality that it would not have been profitable to work it. Slate prospects were mentioned again at the company's meeting in 1905, together with hopes of conveying large quantities of peat and minerals which a syndicate was about to excavate from the moor; but the promised traffic unfortunately failed to materialise.

Two new halts, Snapper Halt for Goodleigh and Caffyns Halt for Golf Course, were erected in 1903 and 1907 respectively. Goodleigh, being a considerable village about three-quarters of a mile from the line, had made many requests for railway facilities to be provided, but the name of Snapper was adopted because an inn (now a house) near the halt, bore that unusual title. Caffyns Halt was intended to serve a golf course that had been laid out upon Caffyns Down, but it was hardly justified as, being situated only a mile from Lynton terminus – the ascent to which required only slightly less effort than the climb to the course direct – the use of the railway did not save any appreciable time for golfers coming from Lynton. The site of the halt, on a grade of 1 in 50, was not a favourable one for train operation, and it is easy to understand why up trains stopped there only when necessary. Parracombe Halt received a welcome addition at about this time in the form of a shelter for waiting passengers; the custom of issuing tickets at the village Post Office continued for some years, however, in spite of the inconvenience caused to strangers who were unaware of the quaint practice.

As in most rural districts before the advent of the motor bus, the inhabitants of the village served by the railway were quite willing to walk a considerable distance to the nearest station. Upon such occasions as Barnstaple market days, for instance, the trains were filled to capacity. Bratton Fleming contributed the bulk of such traffic, and the evening trains, returning with crowds from the market, consisted of six coaches hauled by two locomotives; two coaches and one engine being detached at Bratton and worked back "light" to Barnstaple. A specially noteworthy transport feat was performed in September 1909, when 600 residents of the Lynton district were conveyed to Barnstaple for the Pleasure Fair, one train being made up with two locomotives and nine coaches.

A sad date in the history of this little line was 9th June, 1910, for on that day Sir George Newnes died at his residence, Hollerday House, Lynton. The loss to Lynton and Lynmouth was thus described by the *Exeter Express and Echo*:

"Sir George Newnes was introduced to Lynton in 1885 by Sir Thomas Hewitt. He was at once struck with its beauty and immediately secured a residence there. Since then he has been the best friend the twin villages ever had or ever hope to have.

The extent of his help to Lynton and Lynmouth can never be fully appreciated; in a thousand and one ways he was ready to forward the interests of the towns. Lynton and Lynmouth are separated by a steep cliff, making progress from one village to the other a very difficult matter. One of his first actions was to overcome this difficulty, and to do so he built a cliff railway, the first of its kind in England. He was also the chief promoter of the Lynton and Barnstaple Railway, which, although looked at by many as being anything but a blessing at the time, has since proved that Sir George was right in his opinion, for the railway has proved a great benefit to Lynton and Lynmouth.

So passed a great man who had been successful in many spheres of business, but not so in the railway world; his experience is another illustration that railway working is beset with numerous peculiar difficulties. From first to last, however, Sir George had maintained a belief that the Lynton line would eventually yield a dividend.

Sir Thomas Hewitt, KC, succeeded Sir George as chairman of the company, at a time when the railway was beginning to suffer from severe competition. At the half-yearly meeting in September 1911 he said: "We notice that people travel from Ilfracombe by coach and by coach also from the GWR at Minehead; the boat traffic has developed to the extent of carrying many hundreds of passengers every day, so the shareholders must realise that this takes away their traffic." It should be explained that the words "every day" applied only during the height of the holiday season, and so far as coastal steamers were concerned, only when conditions allowed passengers to be ferried ashore by rowing boats at Lynmouth.

A fatal accident occurred on 26th February, 1913 at Chumhill, between Chelfham and Bratton Fleming, causing the loss of two lives. At about 8 am four men were riding towards Chelfham on a loaded ballast truck, when the wagon gained such momentum on the falling grade that it could not be checked by the brake and, leaving the metals at a sharp curve, turned completely over into a field twenty feet below. The two men who were not killed escaped with injuries, and they attributed the accident to wet leaves having made the rails slippery. This was the second and last fatal accident on the railway, the first having occurred at the Braunton Road crossing, Barnstaple, where a gate-keeper was killed in opening the gates for a mail train.

The year 1913 stands out as having marked the beginning of a comparatively prosperous period, with gross recipts of £9,668, working expenses £6,640, and net receipts £3,028. In this year, and until 1921, dividends of ½% were paid in ordinary shares, but in 1922 the net receipts were only £437, and no dividend was paid. The lean years during the War were weathered successfully under Government control, but in the period which followed, with competition from the road increasing rapidly, there appeared little prospect of a dividend being earned. The limited resources of the railway did not allow even for proper maintenance of the line, and the grass-grown track told of the need for economy – a word that had been heard at every half-yearly meeting of the company, although, of course, the line had existed in a condition of extreme frugality since its birth.

During this independent period the railway employed around 60 plus staff and the following is an approximate distribution along the route:

BARNSTAPLE TOWN	1 Signalman and 1 man for casual work at the siding.
BRAUNTON ROAD CROSSING	1 Crossing Keeper

PILTON WORKS	1 Foreman
	1 Carriage and Wagon Repairer
	1 Carpenter
	1 Carriage Cleaner
	2 Painters
	1 Blacksmith
	2 Apprentices
PILTON YARD	2 Signalmen
	1 Goods Clerk
	1 Goods Porter
(Office)	1 General Manager
	3 Clerks
(Running Staff)	3 Drivers (4 during summer)
	3 Firemen (4 during summer)
	2 Passenger Guards
	1 Spare Guard
(Permanent Way)	1 Permanent Way Inspector
	Platelayers (approximately 18)
	1 Signal and Telegraph Linesman
CHELFHAM	1 Porter Signalman
WOODY BAY	1 Stationmaster
	1 Porter (summer season only)
BRATTON FLEMING	1 Stationmaster
BLACKMOOR	1 Stationmaster
	1 Porter
LYNTON	1 Stationmaster
	1 Warehouseman
	1 Porter (plus one extra during summer)

Early in 1919 Sir Thomas Hewitt resigned the chairmanship of the company, and the directors elected Col. E.B. Jeune, JP, to fill the position. Four years later, in January 1923, Sir Thomas died, the loss to the railway and the neighbourhood being felt keenly by those who had shared with him the task of carrying on the affairs of the company. Unlike the first chairman he had lived to hear that railway grouping was imminent and may have hoped, therefore, that a brighter future awaited the railway.

Reference has been made to the difficulty of climbing to the station at Lynton before the construction of a new road in the 1920s. For vehicles the only route, a mile long, had been via Castle Hill, Lynbridge Road and Lynbridge Hill, where one left the Barnstaple Road to turn sharp right up Station Hill. A much shorter route was available to the pedestrian, however, the suitably-named Shamble Way sheering straight up the hill from Lynton in the manner of a pack-horse track, which it may well have been at one time. Part of the "Way", with its gradient of about 1 in 4, was paved so as to form a path, but the remainder was left in a natural rough state to afford foothold for the ponies that carried, pannier-fashion, mails and the lighter kinds of luggage. A hand-rail, secured to the rocky wall on one side, enabled the less stalwart travellers to rest during their climb, or to steady themselves on the descent.

For many years the first glimpse of Lynton and its impressive coastline was obtained by Railway passengers as they made their way down this difficult path. In daylight the prospect was indeed of exceptional beauty, but after sunset, with the lights of Lynton and, far below, those of Lynmouth in its wooded glen, formed a scene not easily forgotten. With an abundant water supply obtained from the hills, the villages were among the first places in the Country to generate their own electricity, a form of progressiveness to which no-one could object.

Lynton & Barnstaple Railway. Working Time Table.

JUNE, 1908, or until further notice.

DOWN	1		Mondays only. 2		3		4		5		Fridays only. 6				SUNDAYS.	
	arr	dep	arr	dep	arr	dep	arr	dep	arr	dep	arr	dep			arr	dep
Barnstaple {Pilton Yd / Town		a.m. 6 5		a.m. 8 45		a.m. 10 40		p.m. 12 18		p.m. 4 15		p.m.				a.m. 7 15
	6 7	6 20	8 47	9 5	10 2	10 30	12 20	12 38	4 17	4 40		5 33			7 17	7 30
Snapper		6 30		9 15		10 40		12 48		4 50		5 43				7 41
Chelfham	6 39	6 40	9 24	9 25	10 49	10 50	12 57	12 58	5 0	5 1	5 52	5 53			7 51	7 52
Bratton	6 55	6 57	9 40	9 42	11 4	11 5	1 12	1 13	5 16	5 17	6 8	6 9			8 6	8 7
Blackmoor	7 15	7 18	9 59	10 0	11 22	11 23	1 30	1 31	5 34	5 35	6 26	6 27			8 25	8 26
Parracombe		7 30		10 12		11 35		1 43		5 47		6 39				8 38
Woody Bay	7 36	7 38	10 18	10 19	11 41	11 42	1 49	1 50	5 53	5 55	6 45	6 47			8 44	8 46
LYNTON	7 53		10 34		11 57		2 4		6 10		7 2				9 2	

October, 1910, or until further notice.

DOWN	1		Mondays, Wednesdays & Fridays only. 2		3		Tuesdays, Thursdays & Saturdays only. 4		5		Fridays only. 6		7	8	SUNDAYS.	
	arr	dep	arr	dep	arr	dep	arr	dep	arr	dep	arr	dep			arr	dep
Barnstaple {Pilton Yd / Town		a.m. 6 5		a.m. 8 45		a.m. 10 40		p.m. 12 18		p.m. 4 15		p.m. 6 33				a.m. 7 15
	6 7	6 20	8 47	9 5	10 2	10 30	12 20	12 38	4 17	4 40	6 35	6 53			7 17	7 30
Snapper Halt		6 30		9 15		10 40		12 48		4 50						7 40
Chelfham	6 39	6 40	9 24	9 25	10 49	10 50	12 57	12 58	4 59	5 1	7 11	7 12			7 49	7 50
Bratton	6 55	6 57	9 40	9 42	11 4	11 5	1 12	1 13	5 16	5 17	7 26	7 27			8 4	8 5
Blackmoor	7 15	7 18	9 59	10 0	11 22	11 23	1 30	1 31	5 34	5 35	7 43	7 44			8 22	8 23
Parracombe H'lt		7 30		10 12		11 35		1 43		5 47		7 56				8 35
Woody Bay	7 36	7 38	10 18	10 19	11 41	11 42	1 49	1 50	5 53	5 55	8 1	8 2			8 41	8 42
LYNTON	7 53		10 34		11 57		2 4		6 10		8 17				8 57	

Chapter Seven

The Southern Railway

The last milestone in the affairs of the company, as a separate concern, was reached at the meeting in March 1923, at which the Lynton & Barnstaple Railway Company accepted the conditions of purchase by the Southern (LSWR) for £39,267; a paragraph in the *Western Morning News* thus related the event:

> The Lynton & Barnstaple Railway Company, at a meeting held yesterday in London, passed a resolution approving that part of the L&SWR Bill containing the conditions of transfer of the L&BR. Sir Frank Newnes presided and there were also present Sir Edward Mountain, Mr C.E. Roberts Chanter (Solicitor) and Mr Charles E. Drewett (Manager).
>
> Sir Frank Newnes moved a resolution of regret at the death of Sir Thomas Hewitt and apreciation of his valuable and untiring services to the company during many years. This was carried, and Sir Frank referred also to Mr Drewett's twenty-two years' association with the railway. It was the intention of the directors to buy him a little present in recognition of his loyal services.

Mr Drewett, on being relieved of his duties, took up his residence at Barnstaple.

The Southern Railway immediately carried out a number of improvements on the line, including the complete re-ballasting and re-sleepering of the road, and the replacement of rail spikes by sole plates, bolts and clips. Fencing also received attention; previously cattle on the line caused frequent delay to trains. New signals were installed, station accommodation enlarged, and train working improved. A new locomotive, similar to those supplied by Messrs Manning, Wardle & Co. at the opening of the line, was ordered from the same firm and received the name *Lew* (Southern No. E188, makers' No. 2042). The original engines were numbered E759 *Yeo*, E760 *Exe*, E761 *Taw*, and E762 *Lyn*. *Lyn* retained a copper-topped chimney until January 1927, when it returned from Eastleigh adorned with a "stovepipe" chimney, giving it a distinctive appearance. Fortunately, none of the other locomotives was sent to Eastleigh, although their boilers were repaired there.

The passenger coaches were overhauled and equipped with upholstery, new goods vehicles were constructed, and two cranes, mounted on bogies, were brought into use – one as a breakdown crane at Barnstaple, and the other as yard crane at Lynton. They were built by Chambers, Scott & Co., and were capable of lifting 4½ tons at 11ft 6in radius and 3 tons at 15 ft radius. Mounted on two four-wheel bogies with brake gear, they weighed 11 tons. Most of the coaches were fitted with steam heating, but the original acetylene lighting continued to give such excellent service that it was not

General Arrangement drawing for No. 2042 *Lew*.
Courtesy, Hunslet (Holdings) PLC

replaced. An interesting, though unsuccessful, experiment was made with concrete sleepers, but it was found that, in addition to causing noisy running, they lacked the elasticity of the timber variety. They continued in use at stations, however, and a length of straight track near Blackmoor remained equipped with them. Publicity, also, was not overlooked, for a description of a journey over the line was included in the attractive guide *Devon and Cornish Days*, by E.P. Leigh-Bennett, published by the Southern Railway.

You will get to Barnstaple Town in time for an early cup of tea, which will be ready for you on the platform. You will be glad of this because you will have got out of your big corridor coach here, which has carried you smoothly all day, and tea is certainly indicated. There is a change of trains. A change of a most astonishing and amusing kind. Sitting complacently at the opposite side of your platform, looking rather self-conscious because you are staring incredulously at it, is what appears to you a toy train. A tall man could lean his arms on the carriage tops. But it has a blustering little engine up in front which seems impatient to depart; and they are in fact busy round the little guard's van with your luggage. So you laugh and get into it.

"The laughter, however, soon turns to voluble admiration which lasts for over an hour. In no other train have you ever been taken through such excitingly lovely country, or round such Swiss Alpine bends. It goes rather slowly with you, for which you are profoundly thankful, because if it rushed along, like its huge main-line colleagues, you wouldn't be able to feast your eyes on the scenery, as you are doing. Delightful little stations it stops at, too – Snapper Halt, Chelfham, Bratton Fleming, Blackmoor, Parracombe Halt, Woody Bay. The bumptious little engine gives vent to a falsetto shriek of pride on approaching and leaving all of them. Perfect!

Meanwhile the scenery. Why hasn't somebody told you about it? The little foothills, copse covered; the panicky streams hurrying to catch the ebbing tide; two pale amber sheep dogs coercing a flock of harassed dun-covered sheep in a red and green lane; the mouse-coloured thatch crowning china-white cottage walls; an orange jumper hanging out of a window to dry. To the left the regal gesture of the Devon hills; to the right the rugged tableland of Exmoor, the home of the wild red deer. Suddenly, on a stream's bank, a little fence made of the backs of iron bedsteads! This stream is within six feet of us, and the salmon know it well. We keep on going round corners. Now we are alongside a motor road – speed merchants smile at us and win; let them! – now we go slap through the middle of a wood, embroidered with rhododendrons and hyacinths. Now we skim round the fat side of a hill; a sheep dog gallops along the sleepers behind us, livid with expostulation at our trespass. Now comes the first hint of sea; there is a look about those downs, an infallible sign. At one moment a chocolate-covered field is level with our eyes; the next we are searching the heart of a valley deep below. Woody Bay – "tickets please" – and the Lynton, all too soon, 700 feet above the sea.

All these improvements were insufficient to secure the line against the effects of steadily increasing competition from the road, which itself had been improved greatly by the construction of a new length at Parracombe, eliminating two hills with gradients of 1 in 4; the railway, owing to its many inherent limitations, was unable to reply with a still better service, and local support almost vanished. The line remained a great favourite with holiday-makers, many of whom have since lamented its passing, but the extent and sincerity of local feeling may be gauged from the fact that, although a meeting was held at Barnstaple to oppose the closing of the line, all the delegates from Lynton arrived by car. Words could not hold much meaning when preceded by such a practical demonstration.

The closing was, of course, regretted, even when it is realised that a railway must be an economic proposition, no matter how charming its setting. We have seen that this line was unable to compete with the horse brake and the earliest motor car; how, then, could it hope to rival modern roads unless freed from its hampering restrictions? An unfortunate combination of gauge, gradient, and curve rendered further improvement impossible. Those who are familiar with North Devon appreciate that it is at a disadvantage geographically in approaching Lynton from the south-west, for the more logical, if more difficult, route from the east is negotiated successfully by its rubber-tyred competitors. From the economic standpoint, therefore, there was every justification for the Southern's action in closing the line. But the news that the track, locomotives, rolling stock, and materials were to be sold by auction came as a shock to many, for the hope that a local interest might yet take over the line still existed and was freely discussed.

Manning Wardle 2–6–2T Modifications to SR E188 *Lew*.

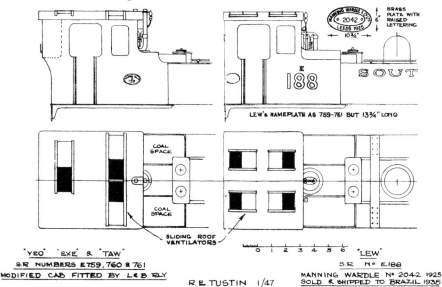

Chapter Eight
The Closing and Sale

About 300 people took the opportunity of travelling over the railway for the last time on Sunday 29th September, 1935. The weather, which had been very unsettled, was fair, and an even greater number of passengers was anticipated by the locomotive authorities, who had prepared four locomotives and two trains in readiness; one train of nine coaches sufficed, however, with engines 188 *Lew* and 759 *Yeo* in charge; but the joyous atmosphere of the occasion was only apparent and was not shared by all the passengers, many of whom were feeling anything but cheerful. Familiar views were appreciated all the more eagerly because of the inevitable absence, in future, of the faithful little train.

The last train was worked in each direction by engine 188 leading and engine 759 train engine, together with nine coaches. Driver Cording and Fireman F. Worth were on the leading engine and Driver W. Worth and Fireman Heale were on the second engine. The guard of the train was Porter Guard Walkey and the train was accompanied by Mr E.S Moore, the Western Divisional Locomotive Running Superintendent, Southern Railways Detective Sergt Grant, Detective Labdon and A.E. Edwards. In addition, Mr Nunn, the Divisional Superintendent, together with the station-master, were at Barnstaple Town to see the departure of the train. The last ticket issued at Lynton was a third single from Lynton to Woody Bay.

The return journey was made throughout in darkness and in rain, to the accompaniment of much whistling and exploding of detonators, with *Lew* again leading. North Walk appeared to be a solid mass of cheering people who, despite the pouring rain, had left their homes to wave a last welcome to the train.

During the days which followed, engineers' and material trains were worked to Pilton yard, conveying stock in readiness for the sale. Several pieces of machinery from the Pilton shops destined for Eastleigh were placed on open wagons, worked round to the transfer siding at Barnstaple Town, and loaded into standard-gauge wagons.

Gradually the sidings and even the running lines at Pilton became filled with running stock. It was a depressing spectacle, contrasting sharply with the scenes of activity that had taken place there daily for so many years – the preparation of the engines for their turns and the marshalliing of trains in proper order. On examination the vehicles were seen to bear certain signs – "Lot 52", "Lot 17", and so on; the depressing sign had been applied even to the track and the locomotives.

As the day of the sale approached prospective purchasers came to inspect the lots, but there were also others who, without commercial

SOUTHERN RAILWAY

Closing of Lynton and Barnstaple Light Railway

The Southern Railway announce that they will cease to operate the Lynton and Barnstaple Light Railway on and from September 30th, 1935. In place thereof arrangements have been made to afford satisfactory alternative services for the conveyance of passengers, parcels, goods and mineral traffic by road transport.

The Southern National. Omnibus Company will convey passengers and their luggage between the area served by this line and Barnstaple Junction. Through Rail—Road tickets will be issued as follows :—

To	From
Chelfham	Lynton
Bratton Fleming	
Blackmoor	
Parracombe	
Woody Bay	
Lynton	

Passengers' accompanied luggage will be conveyed free, subject to the usual conditions. For particulars of times see other announcements.

Messrs. Chaplins Ltd., the accredited Agents of the Southern Railway, will undertake the delivery and collection of parcels and merchandise traffic, including coal and mineral traffic, between Barnstaple and Lynton and the intermediate points. Particulars of the charges for such services and information respecting the Local Agents who will be appointed can be obtained upon application to the Divisional Superintendent, Exeter Central, or the Station Master, Barnstaple.

Waterloo Station, S.E. 1,
September, 1935.

H. A. WALKER,
General Manager.

C.X. 2840/ 6⁄9985

Printed in England.
• Waterlow & Sons Limited, London and Dunstable

motives, had come to view and photograph for the last time the now unwanted railway, still recalling memories of happy holidays. To them, the announcement that alternative road services would be available conveyed no comfort at all.

Quite a crowd thronged the yard and shops on the morning of Wednesday 13th November, 1935, some people tapping this, others measuring that, to the disgust of the line's late patrons, whose hopes of successful bidding did not rise above the acquisition of a souvenir. The sale, timed to commence at 11 am, was held in the old carriage shed, and was prefaced by an announcement from the auctioneer to the effect that the locomotive name-plates were to be removed for presentation to the Railway Museum at York. The first three lots consisted of track, the bidding for which was so discouraging that they were withdrawn at two shillings a yard; this was accompanied, of course, by a murmur of approval from the enthusiasts. Next came the 2–6–2 locomotive *Lew* which, after brisk bidding, was sold for £52; the sister engines *Yeo* and *Taw* fetched £50 each, but *Exe*, with a steel firebox, failed to get more than £34. The spare boiler for these locomotives, with copper firebox, fetched £20. After some more spares came the engine *Lyn*, attaining £50, followed by the coaches at prices varying from £9 to £13 10s. 0d. each, 8-wheel goods vehicles from £6 10s. 0d. to £9 10s. 0d., and 4-wheel trucks from £3 15s. 0d. (open) and £4 (covered). The two portable hand jib cranes sold at £30 and £29 each, and the one jib truck for £6 10s. 0d. The remaining 136 lots consisted of various materials and spares; but lot 200, at Lynton station, must be mentioned. "Boarded and glazed signal cabin, two sectional concrete cabins, 7-lever signal frame, 2 double signal posts with ladders and fittings, about 300 feet signal rods (?) with rollers and pedestals, 3 cast iron lamp posts, and the telegraph wiring on concrete and wood posts from Lynton to the 15½-mile post." This assortment, which was typical of the station lots, was sold for £7. The turntable from Pilton was acquired by the Romney, Hythe & Dymchurch Railway.

The weeks that followed the sale were even more saddening. The rumour that four locomotives had been purchased merely as scrap proved to be true, and strong fellows armed with sledge hammers and oxy-acetylene cutting apparatus fell to upon the engines, so that in a few days four heaps of debris were all that remained of four smart, well-kept locomotives. Men were at work also upon the rolling stock, salvaging only the metal fittings from the bodies and chassis, the timber being disposed of in bonfires.

One of *Lyn's* name-plates has been preserved by one of the railway's friends who resided at Weston-super-Mare; and proclaimed the name of his residence and formed a noteworthy combination of affection and utility.

The removal of the track was undertaken by Mr S. Castle of Furze-hatt, Plymstock, South Devon. The "wrecking train" was worked by *Lew*, the only locomotive to escape destruction at the hands of the scrap-metal merchants, and was made up with a bogie brake van, two open wagons for sleepers, and one flat bogie wagon for rails. Incle-ment weather hampered operations for the first few weeks, and *Lew* itself was pressed to capacity in hauling the heavy loads over the poorly maintained road, but as the weather improved work pro-ceeded rapidly. Commencing operations at Lynton, the demolition gang worked to the following method: one man slacked off fish-bolts and rail fastenings, leaving sufficient only to ensure that the track was safe for the passage of the train at reduced speed; behind the train fish-bolts and plates were removed from a pair of rails, then the inside rail fastenings; a bar was inserted in the empty fish-bolt holes and with the aid of a few blows from a sledge-hammer the rails were tilted out of the outside clips. The rails were then lifted and run on to the next flat wagon (about eleven tons of rails making one load). Next, the sleepers were lifted by means of a pick, to be stacked on end in the open wagons. The train then moved forward one rail-length and the sequence of operations was repeated. Rails were cut into short lengths at Barnstaple and loaded into standard gauge wagons.

When this dismal task of demolition was completed *Lew* returned to Messrs Manning, Wardle & Co., for overhaul and minor alterations to fit her for service in the plantations of Brazil. It was good to know that one, at any rate, of the locomotives had avoided annihilation, although not one of the original engines; but it is sad to reflect that her stable companions would have travelled with *Lew* had their purchasers not acted so hastily.

Three carriages, however, were preserved intact. Two (Nos. 6991 and 6993) came to rest on lengths of line at Snapper, and the third (No. 6992) was taken by road to Clannaborough Rectory, Copple-stone. The underframes of the remaining coaches, and all metal underframes of goods rolling stock, accompanied *Lew* to Brazil.

Such, then, was the end of the saleable parts of the popular "Lyn-ton line"; but there will remain for centuries earthworks to show where once lay the path over which the faithful *Yeo, Exe, Taw, Lyn*, and *Lew* hauled their train loads of happy passengers.

The station buildings and properties were sold and recorded by Mr Hayward who attended the sale, in a letter to the author in 1938;

> The Pilton property was sold for about £3,000 to a Mr J. Sanders (the son of the original wool merchants) and he told me that the Railway had such arbitary powers that they cut right through Messrs Sanders premises,

acquired the living house, ran them into an expensive law case and Sanders only came out with about £600 of which at least £350 went on law costs; it is rather strange that the son of the original owner comes once again into possession, and he may cover himself later as some 20 feet or so will be required for road widening purposes; Mr Sanders showed me photos of the old garden which extended across where the turntable was and over to that cob wall.

Bratton station sold for £100, Blackmoor station for £700, Woody Bay station for £405, but Lynton was withdrawn at £475 and Chelfham at £275. In the case of Chelfham one has to take some liability in regard to the viaduct so that it is no wonder that purchasers are wary.

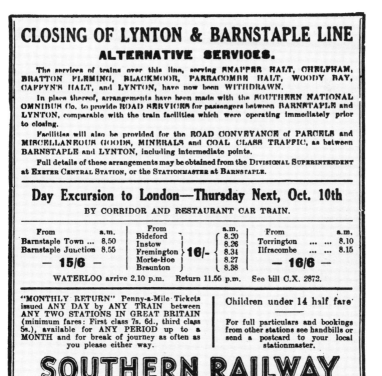

CLOSING OF LYNTON & BARNSTAPLE LINE

ALTERNATIVE SERVICES.

The services of trains over this line, serving SNAPPER HALT, CHELFHAM, BRATTON FLEMING, BLACKMOOR, PARRACOMBE HALT, WOODY BAY, CAFFYN'S HALT, and LYNTON, have now been WITHDRAWN.

In place thereof, arrangements have been made with the SOUTHERN NATIONAL OMNIBUS Co. to provide ROAD SERVICES for passengers between BARNSTAPLE and LYNTON, comparable with the train facilities which were operating immediately prior to closing.

Facilities will also be provided for the ROAD CONVEYANCE of PARCELS and MISCELLANEOUS GOODS, MINERALS and COAL CLASS TRAFFIC, as between BARNSTAPLE and LYNTON, including intermediate points.

Full details of these arrangements may be obtained from the DIVISIONAL SUPERINTENDENT at EXETER CENTRAL STATION, or the STATIONMASTER at BARNSTAPLE.

Day Excursion to London—Thursday Next, Oct. 10th
BY CORRIDOR AND RESTAURANT CAR TRAIN.

From	a.m.	From		a.m.	From	a.m.
Barnstaple Town	8.50	Bideford		8.20	Torrington	8.10
Barnstaple Junction	8.55	Instow		8.26	Ilfracombe	8.15
— 15/6 —		Fremington	16/-	8.31	— 16/6 —	
		Morte-Hoe		8.27		
		Braunton		8.38		

WATERLOO arrive 2.10 p.m.   Return 11.55 p.m.   See bill C.X. 2872.

"MONTHLY RETURN" Penny-a-Mile Tickets issued ANY DAY by ANY TRAIN between ANY TWO STATIONS IN GREAT BRITAIN (minimum fares: First class 7s. 6d., third class 5s.), available for ANY PERIOD up to a MONTH and for break of journey as often as you please either way.

Children under 14 half fare

For full particulars and bookings from other stations see handbills or send a postcard to your local stationmaster.

SOUTHERN RAILWAY

DISMANTLEMENT SALE

of the Track, Rolling Stock and Materials of the

LYNTON AND BARNSTAPLE RAILWAY.

By Order of the Directors of the SOUTHERN RAILWAY CO.

CATALOGUE

OF THE

RAILWAY TRACK, LOCOMOTIVES, ROLLING STOCK & MATERIALS,

INCLUDING

16¾ MILES TRACK

23¼-in. GAUGE, 40-lb. F.B. RAILS on 4-ft. 6-in. CREOSOTED SLEEPERS with POINTS AND CROSSINGS,

SIGNAL AND TELEGRAPH APPARATUS,

FIVE TANK LOCOMOTIVES,

Four by MANNING-WARDLE and One by BALDWIN,

SEVENTEEN 8-WHEEL PASSENGER CARRIAGES,

NINETEEN OPEN GOODS WAGONS (4 to 8 TONS),

TEN COVERED GOODS WAGONS,

THREE 8-TON GOODS BRAKE VANS,

PLATELAYERS' TROLLEYS, TURNTABLE,

PORTABLE CRANES, WEIGHBRIDGE,

REPAIR SHOP EQUIPMENT,

INCLUDING

ENGINEERS' AND SMITHS' TOOLS,   TANGYE 14-H.P. GAS ENGINE,

STORES AND MATERIALS,

STATION AND OFFICE FURNITURE AND OTHER EFFECTS,

Which will be offered for Sale by Auction by Messrs.

FULLER HORSEY, SONS & CASSELL

AT THE

PILTON DEPOT, BARNSTAPLE,

On WEDNESDAY, NOVEMBER 13th, 1935,

At ELEVEN O'CLOCK precisely.

May be viewed on production of Catalogue to be obtained of

F. H. WILLIS, Esq., Secretary to the Southern Railway Co., Waterloo Station, London, S.E.; or of Messrs. FULLER, HORSEY, SONS & CASSELL, Auctioneers, 11, Billiter Square, Fenchurch Street, London, E.C.3.   Tel. Monument 0081.

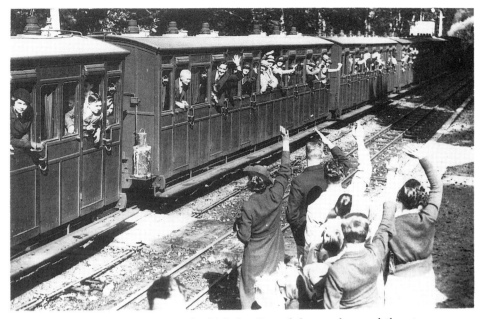

The last down train shows the high loading of the coaches and the atmosphere that prevailed. It was a pity the utilisation of the service was not as that of the last day, it might just have saved the Lynton and Barnstaple Railway from closure!   *Lens of Sutton*

The last journey of the Lynton and Barnstaple Railway after 40 years of service. This was witnessed by large crowds including many who had been at the opening of this line. Due to the heavy demand it was necessary to have two engines hauling the train.   *Author's collection*

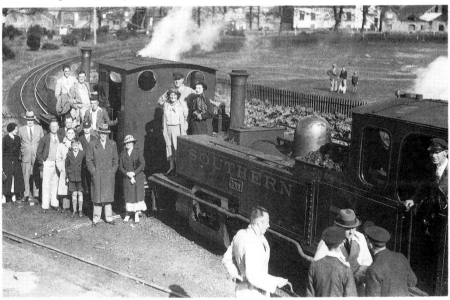

Scenes of demolition in 1936 when the track was lifted. The top right view shows one of the coaches left on a section of rail as a summer house at Snapper Halt. *R.W. Kidner*

Appendix One

Locomotive Working

Notes supplied by the late Frank E. Box

The down journey to Lynton always seemed the more interesting, as it was nearly all "collar" work on the climb up from sea level, while in the case of the up trips, after Blackmoor, it was mostly a matter of brakes and not of locomotive work.

The engines invariably worked chimney first to Lynton and cab first to Barnstaple, and – it may have been fancy – it struck me that some at least of the engines worked better – with a healthier "beat" – in forward than in reversing gear.

I have prepared tables showing 10 runs in each direction; the first 5 runs in each table have been chosen to illustrate good performances by each of the 5 locomotives.

RUN No. 1 is the best of my pre-grouping records.

RUN No. 2 with *Exe* and a light load provided both the fastest overall time and the fastest running time I have noted. The "stop" at Snapper was remarkable, for the train was actually at a standstill for a fraction of a second only.

The intermediate running times between Barnstaple and Bratton, although good, have been beaten by *Yeo*, but from Bratton to Lynton they are easily the fastest I have recorded.

RUN 3. *Taw* on the Sunday excursion had an easy task with a light load and only 4 stops. The time, 25 mins 42 secs, to Bratton, the first stop, was good.

RUN 4 was with *Lyn*, the 2–4–2T Baldwin engine.

RUN 5 with *Lew* is a record of a trip made by the only post-grouping engine.

RUN 6. *Yeo* did excellent work on the morning mail in recovering time.

RUN 7, again with *Yeo*, was made on the Wednesday before the closing, and considerable time was spent at the several stations during which a travelling staff unfastened trade advertisements to be picked up on the return trip. Time so spent was more than regained by the engine.

RUN 8, again with *Yeo*, carried the last rail-borne mails to Lynton. The gross load with 16 tons of coal, was some 45 tons, and with a slippery rail a good performance was put up.

RUN 9, with *Lyn* and *Lew*, is an example of work with a double-headed train, the gross load being about 60 tons.

RUN 10 is that of the final down journey on Sunday, 29th September, 1935. Four engines, *Yeo, Exe, Taw* and *Lew*, had steam raised at Pilton in readiness for dealing with any number of passengers – up to the capacity of the 17 coaches possessed by the line – who might have presented themselves. One train of 9 coaches, the maximum load for 2 engines, however, proved sufficient for the 300 or so travellers.

With a gross load of about 100 tons the running time for the journey was 76 minutes. On the fairly level stretch before Snapper the two locomotives ran one quarter mile in $39\frac{3}{5}$ secs, 23 miles per hour, and steadily plodded up the long 1 in 50 to Blackmoor at a little under 15 miles per hour, the 3 miles between mile-posts 8 and 11 taking 12 mins 21 secs, with a maximum of 15.3 mph at milepost 9.

I have referred to some fast times made by *Yeo* between Barnstaple and Bratton, and brief details may be interesting.

In 1933 with 2 coaches, $17\frac{3}{4}$ tons tare, this engine ran from Chelfham to Bratton, 3 miles of 1 in 50 up, in 11 mins dead; two years later, with 3 coaches and 1 bogie van, 33 tons tare, it ran from Barnstaple to the stop at Snapper in 8 mins exactly, and thence to Chelfham in 6 mins 12 secs, 21 mph being attained on the 1 in 50 up approaching the viaduct.

On another occasion a maximum of $26\frac{1}{2}$ mph was recorded with this engine at mile-post $2\frac{1}{4}$.

In the case of up trains, *Exe* again provides the fastest running time, 68 mins 13 secs. She was lightly loaded, and had been held at Blackmoor for 23 minutes for crossing purposes.

There is not much to be said about the locomotive work on the homeward journey – run 20 – on the last day. Much steam had been used for the duet played on the engine's whistles at each stopping place, and, as no water had been taken en route, and coal was running short, it was with some relief that the responsible locomotive staff saw the train safely shedded at Pilton that night. The actual departure and arrival time at Lynton and Barnstaple were 7 hrs 58 mins 30 secs (due 7.55 pm) and 9 hrs 37 mins 28 secs (due 9.22 pm); 16 minutes had been spent at the stations, including 8 minutes at Blackmoor for press photographic purposes.

Lynton and Barnstaple Railway. UP.

Engine Driver's Report. _141_ day. _Sep. 19 enter_ 190 _1_ _6-45_ Train.

STATIONS.	Service Time.		Actual Time.		Vehicles Attached.					Vehicles Detached.		REMARKS.
	Arrival.	Departure.	Arrival.	Departure.	Coaches.	Brake Vans.	Goods. Goods Trucks Loaded.		Empty.	Goods Trucks 8 W.	4 W.	
	H.	M.	H.	M.	H.	M.	H.	M.							
Lynton					6·45	2						
Wooda Bay					7·10	7·5						
Blackmoor					7·24	7·25						
Bratton					7·41	7·43						
Chelfham					7·58	8·0						
Barnstaple					8·20							

_J. C. ...._ Driver's Signature.

Sample of the driver's Report form.

DOWN TRAINS

	1	2	3	4	5
Date.	28.8.1918	10.9.1932	26.5.1935	31.7.1935	20.9.1935
Train.	4.30 p.m.	4.30 p.m.	11.50 a.m. Sunday.	3.15 p.m.	3.15 p.m.
Engine.	YEO.	760 EXE.	761 TAW.	762 LYN.	188 LEW.
Load.	4 coaches.	2 coaches.	2 coaches.	3 coaches.	4 coaches.
Tare.	35¼ tons.	17¼ tons.	17¼ tons.	26¼ tons.	35¼ tons.

Distance M. Ch.	Station	1 arr M.S.	1 dep M.S.	2 arr M.S.	2 dep M.S.	3 arr M.S.	3 dep M.S.	4 arr M.S.	4 dep M.S.	5 arr M.S.	5 dep M.S.
— —	Barnstaple Town	—	0 0	—	0 0	—	0 0	—	0 0	—	0 0
— 30	Pilton Yard						1 41		2 11*		1 58*
2 54	Snapper Halt	10 2	10 42	9 26	9 26*	8 15	8 58	10 20	10 32	9 21	9 32
4 54	Chelfham	18 53	20 35 W	16 5	16 43	—	15 26 (Pass)	17 52	19 47	17 9	18 38 W
7 54	Bratton Fleming	32 58	34 25	27 52	28 21	25 42	26 18	32 52	34 44	30 10	31 40
11 62	Blackmoor	51 17	52 8	41 44	42 23	40 47	44 12	50 36	54 34 X	47 19	51 19 X
14 33	Parracombe Halt	61 51	63 14	50 47	54 54	52 38	56 0 W	64 14	68 48	61 0	65 55 W
15 77	Woody Bay	69 59	74 52 T	60 30	63 38 T	62 1	62 45	73 58	76 45	72 27	74 0
17 35	Caffyns Halt			68 10	68 31	—	68 33 (Pass)	82 34	83 25	79 53	80 15
19 23	Lynton	86 3	—	74 23	—	74 38	—	90 19	—	87 45	—
	Running Time		75 7		65 1		66 31		74 10		73 45

Notes:

2. *Momentary stop only at Snapper.

4. (= 73¾ min. net) *Signals approaching Pilton.

5. (= 73¾ mins. net) *Signals approaching Pilton.

67

		6		7		8		9		10	
Date.		6.4.1935.		25.9.1935		28.9.1935		5.9.1934		29.9.1935 Sunday.	
Train.		5.33 a.m. Mail.		10.15 a.m.		5.33 a.m. Mail.		10.15 a.m.		11.50 a.m.	
Engine.		759 YEO.		759 YEO.		759 YEO.		762 LYN. 188 LEW.		188 LEW. 759 YEO.	
Load.		2 coaches and 2 bogie vans.		3 coaches and 1 bogie van.		2 coaches and 2 loaded bogie coal waggons.		5 coaches and 1 bogie van.		9 coaches.	
Tare.		29¼ tons.		33 tons.		29 tons.		50½ tons.		80 tons.	
		arr.	dep.	arr.	dep.	arr.	dep.	arr.	dep.	arr.	dep.
Distance M. Ch.		M. S.	M. S.	M. S.	M. S.	M. S.	M. S.	M. S.	M. S.	M. S.	M. S.
— —	Barnstaple Town...	—	0 0	—	0 0	—	0 0	—	0 0	—	0 0
— 30	Pilton Yard	2 22	*13 18	—	1 57	2 16	2 16	1 55	—	9 9	47 (P)
2 54	Snapper Halt	21	28 (P)	8 5	9 59	10	12 (P)	9 49	10 14	16 56	W 21 24
4 54	Chelfham	28	45 (P)	16 34	X 21 19	17	56 (P)	18 9	X 20 25	34 29	36 48
7 54	Bratton Fleming...	39 32	40 41	32 32	36 42	30 28	31 58	33 3	38 22	53 51	58 23
11 62	Blackmoor	56 5	†60 31	53 41	56 35	50 29	51 38	54 53	58 28	67 44	W 72 21
14 33	Parracombe Halt...	69 3	W 72 29	65 52	W 69 49	60 21	W 64 53	68 40	W 73 7	79 17	80 49
15 77	Woody Bay	78 20	79 7	76 18	77 18	71 11	71 35	79 29	T 83 11	86	38 (P)
17 35	Caffyns Halt	84	1 (Pass)	82 12	83 3	76	53 (P)	88 55	*89 13	92 25	*93 26
19 23	Lynton ...	89 40	—	89 2	—	82 30	—	95 27 / 97 19	96 20	94 29	—
	Running Time ...	M. S. 68 56 (= 68 mins. net.)		M. S. 69 31		M. S. 74 55		M. S. 76 24		M. S. 76 0	

*Signal stop at Pilton. †2 vans detached.

*Stop outside Lynton to detach pilot engine. (trains 9 and 10)

W = Engine took water.   T = Tickets collected.   X = Crossed up train.   P = Pass.

UP TRAINS.

	Distance M. Ch.	11 arr.	11 dep.	12 arr.	12 dep.	13 arr.	13 dep.	14 arr.	14 dep.	15 arr.	15 dep.
Date.		10.9.1932		22.9.1933		6.4.1935		13.4.1935		31.7.1935	
Train.		7.13 a.m.		9.25 a.m.		7.13 a.m.		6.7 p.m.		6.7 p.m.	
Engine.		760 EXE.		761 TAW.		759 YEO.		188 LEW.		761 LYN.	
Load.		2 coaches.		3 coaches and 1 4-wh. truck.		2 coaches and 1 bogie van.		2 coaches.		3 coaches.	
Tare.		17¾ tons.		29¾ tons.		24 tons.		17¾ tons.		26¼ tons.	
		M. S.	M. S.	M. S.	M. S.	M. S.	M. S.	M. S.	M. S.	M. S.	M. S.
Lynton	—	—	0 0	—	0 0	—	0 0	—	0 0	—	0 0
Caffyns Halt	1 68	8	50 (P)	7	46 (P)	7	47 (P)	7 57	8 15	7 42	8 32
Woody Bay	3 26	13 10	14 31	13 7	15 52	13 27	13 39	14 37	15 29	14 46	16 45
Parracombe Halt	4 70	20 0	20 55	21 17	22 59W	18 46	19 5	20 40	26 9	22 25	25 17W
Blackmoor	7 41	30 22	53 34X	32 52	36 11	29 23	32 35	36 33	40 23	34 33	35 39
Bratton Fleming	11 49	68 2	65 7	51 6	53 8	46 35	51 40	53 42	54 45	50 7	51 45
Chelfham	14 49	78	17 (P)	63 38*	82 53X	61 36	66 30X	64 42	67 34	62 7	65 18
Snapper Halt	16 49	85	2 (P)	89 26	90 10	73 59	74 12	74 53	75 8	72 35	72 55
Pilton Yard	18 73	92	26	97	47	82 16	82 25*	83	36	82	35
Barnstaple Town	19 23	93 46	—	99 13	—	84 50	—	85 16	—	84 10	—
		M. s.		M. s.		M. s.		M. s.		M. s.	
Running Time		68 13		70 8		70 46		70 37		71 30	

Column 12: (= 69¼ mins. net.) *Signal stop outside Chelfham from 63.38 to 64.4

Column 13: (= 70 mins. net.) *Signal stop at Pilton.

69

Table of Lynton & Barnstaple Railway train running times (arr./dep. in minutes and seconds, M. s.):

	Distance M. Ch.	16 arr.	16 dep.	17 arr.	17 dep.	18 arr.	18 dep.	19 arr.	19 dep.	20 arr.	20 dep.
Date		20.9.1935		25.9.1935		28.9.1935		8.8.1934		29.9.1935 Sunday.	
Train		6.7 p.m.		12.42 p.m.		9.25 a.m.		6.7 p.m.		7.55 p.m.	
Engine		188 LEW.		759 YEO.		188 LEW.		188 LEW (to Blackmoor only) 761 TAW.		188 LEW, 759 YEO.	
Load		4 coaches.		3 coaches = 28½ tons 1 van added at Blackmoor, and 4 goods vehicles at Bratton. Total tare = 46 tons		3 coaches and 1 four wheeled truck = 29½ tons, 1 bogie truck attached at Woody Bay =		5 coaches.		9 coaches.	
Tare		35¼ tons.				35½ tons.		44¼ tons.		80 tons.	
Lynton	—	—	0 0	—	0 0	—	0 0	—	0 0	—	0 0
Caffyns Halt	1 63	8 40	8 45	7 49	8 13		8 34 (P)	8 4	8 15		10 3 (P)
Woody Bay	3 26	15 9	15 30	13 45	16 58	14 27	19 1	13 56	14 32	17 5	18 18
Parracombe Halt	4 70	20 47	23 20W	22 8	23 32W	24 15	26 9	20 12	22 58W	24 50	26 53
Blackmoor	7 41	33 37	38 16	32 58	37 33	36 42	39 39	32 14	36 51	38 57	46 54
Bratton Fleming	11 49	52 51	54 40	51 36	56 59	55 13	56 34	51 42	53 23	63 20	66 35
Chelfham	14 49	65 12	68 23	67 22	71 0*	67 26	75 48X	63 36	67 28	78 8	79 38
Snapper Halt	16 49	76 9	78 20	78 3	78 14	82 42	82 52	74 48	75 3		87 56 (P)
Pilton Yard	18 73	84 2	84 50*	86 2	86 25	90 2		83 8	83 14	96	96 11
Barnstaple Town	19 23	87 18		89 2		91 23		84 53		98 58	
Running Time		73 41		71 1		72 7		70 34		83 0	

Train 16 — (=72¾ mins. net.) *Signal stop at Pilton.

Train 17 — (= 70 mins. net.) *Signal stop outside Chelfham from 67.22 to 67.53

W = Engine took water. X = Crossed down train.

Principle Lengths of Station Trackwork, etc.

Location	Platforms Up	Platforms Down	Loop	Sidings, etc.
Barnstaple T.	–	326'	408'	Transfer = 368'; top of loop = 130'
Pilton Wharf	–	–	–	Siding to catch point = 162'
Pilton Yard	–	–	568'	Turntable line, table = 30'; lead-in = 105'
				Loco shed 1 = 58'; lead-in = 57'
				Workshop = 72'; loco shed 2 = 61'; lead-in = 124'
				Carriage shed 1 = 153'; lead-in = 125'
				Carriage shed 2 = 157'; lead-in = 105'
				Carriage shed 3 = 158'; lead-in = 104'
				Lead-in from loop to 2 & 3 = 63'
				Goods shed = 36'; lead-in = 224'
				Siding = 203'; lead-in to shed & siding = 102'
				Headshunt = 371'
Snapper Halt	–	132'	–	
Chelfham Via.	–	–	–	336' long
Chelfham	221'	165'	455'	Sidings = 55'
Lancey Brook Viaduct	–	–	–	140' long
Bratton Fleming	204'	204'	416'	Long siding = 250'; short siding = 156'
Blackmoor	216'	186'	428'	Up side, removed 1930 = 156'
				Down side, by platform = 252'
				by stables = 156'
				Headshunt (before lengthening, 1930) = 84'
Parracombe Halt	–	213'	–	
Woody Bay	214'	214'	438'	Siding = 190'; headshunt 229'
Caffyns Halt	132'	–	–	
Lynton	306' (Main)		360'	Goods shed = 40'; siding beyond = 113'
	180' (Bay)			Back siding = 260'; bay siding = 302'
				Loco shed and siding = 321'

Appendix Three

Monthly Engine Mileage
1924 to 1928

Compiled by W.E. Hayward

Extracted and tabulated from the weekly (app.) report sheets that were rendered by W.S. Davey to Mr W. Bale at the Pilton Head-quarters.

Note: It is interesting that the engine names appear on the reports until 30/11/24, from then the numbers only are given; on the report dated 31/7/25 first appears No. 188 *Lew*.

The numbers are generally prefixed by the letter "L".

Engine	Date	a	b	c	d	e	Total
1924							
Yeo	Aug	11380	125	118	544		12167
Exe	"	1203	653	728	670	320	3254
Taw	"	4385	762	559	363	369	6069
Lyn	"	8066	540	615	355	303	9576
Yeo	Sept	848	759	402	240		2249
Exe	"	810	350	290	204		1654
Taw	"	987	656	723	404		2770
Lyn	"	524	139	325	155		1143
Yeo	Oct	575	28	−m−	801		1404
Exe	"	326	342	−m−	—		668
Taw	"	446	593	−m−	445		1484
Lyn	"	10	188	−m−	231		429
Yeo	Nov	123	542	461	369		1495
Exe	"	—	—	—	—		—
Taw	"	359	441	404	163		1367
Lyn	"	315	199	296	170		980
759	Dec	523	373	327	398		1621
760	"	—	—	—	—		—
761	"	191	412	563	407		1573
762	"	407	331	310	39		1087

Total mileage run by each engine for the above five months and including the previous mileage apparently brought forward into the first weekly report for August.

759	Yeo	18,936
760	Exe	5,576
761	Taw	13,263
762	Lyn	13,215

Scenes at Pilton on sale day (including Lot 8 resting forlorn in its shed), and
the sale notice of the station properties offered by John Smale & Co.

R.W. Kidner

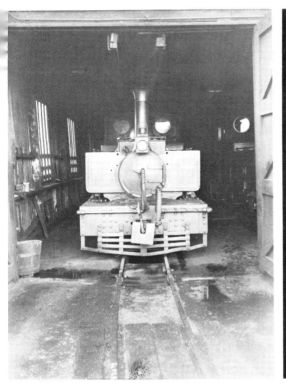

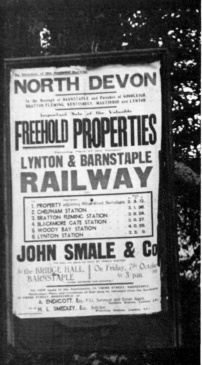

(Left)
The end; a wreath provided by Captain Woolf R.N. of Woody Bay at the buffer stops of Barnstaple station.　　*Author's collection*

(Bottom)
Mr. Baker, who drove the Barnstaple–Lynton horse coach before the railway came, at Bratton Fleming on the closing day.
　　Author's collection

(Below)
Remains of *Lyn* after the sale; a sad sight!　　*R.W. Kidner*

No. 761 *Taw* near Collar Bridge in 1935 with a standard formation train of the time. This view depicts well the scenery and twisting route of the line.

R.W. Kidner

The long, low viaduct of Lancey Brook in a rather remote point on the line. It consisted of masonry piers with steel spans and, after the line closed, was demolished by the Army as an exercise.   *Author's collection*

"From the window", near Dean Steep.   *R.W. Kidner*

A Lynton-bound train rounding the curve near Blackmoor station.
LGRP, courtesy David & Charles

The view from the First class passenger saloon. *Author's collection*

View of Pilton machine shop. *R.W. Kidner*

An L & B Rly official postcard taken at Collar Bridge on a trial train prior to the opening. Note the handpainted name *Taw* on this postcard (which was hand coloured) and No. 4 in the series of 10. *Author's collection*

A view of *Yeo* at Lynton station with an 8-ton bogie brake van next to the engine, followed by one of the open wagons and two coaches. Note another 8-ton bogie in the goods shed and the further two coaches. *Author's collection*

1925

Engine	Date	a	b	c	d	e	Total
759	Jan	595	535	395	253	——	1778
760	„	——	——	——	——	——	——
761	„	290	548	740	464	181	1823
762	„	233	54	——	456	365	1108
759	Feb	——	226	431	404	302	1363
760	„	——	——	——	——	——	——
761	„	215	181	692	583	189	1860
762	„	365	686	163	290	48	1552
759	Mar	321	327	396	415	610	2069
760	„	——	——	——	——	——	——
761	„	190	500	611	581	320	2222
762	„	40	360	122	122	——	644
759	Apl	455	43	——	——	——	498
760	„	24	339	542	732	——	1637
761	„	540	607	581	384	——	2112
762	„	370	87	43	194	——	694
759	May	——	——	——	–m–	——	——
760	„	451	364	542	–m–	——	1355
761	„	498	739	537	–m–	——	1774
762	„	39	55	95	–m–	——	189
759	June	185	584	635	457	475	2336
760	„	173	485	425	607	411	2101
761	„	365	——	——	——	——	365
762	„	43	123	260	126	212	764
759	July	721	735	739	61	——	2256
760	„	536	642	739	995	——	2912
761	„	——	——	——	——	——	——
762	„	420	336	525	533	——	1814
188	„	——	——	——	10	——	10
759	Aug	501	770	332	711	369	2683
760	„	495	611	755	749	491	3101
761	„	——	121	631	540	255	1547
762	„	415	634	498	216	80	1843
188	„	104	——	——	——	258	362
759	Sept	995	655	612	759	——	3021
760	„	994	630	632	269	——	2525
761	„	493	360	173	90	——	1116
762	„	——	——	——	——	——	——
188	„	348	520	323	171	——	1362

759	Oct	385	174	493	865	——	1917
760	"	500	618	581	——	——	1699
761	"	343	237	——	251	——	831
762	"	——	——	——	——	——	——
188	"	——	179	126	669	——	974
759	Nov	359	312	385	336	——	1392
760	"	711	537	480	210	——	1938
761	"	137	122	300	226	——	785
762	"	——	——	——	——	——	——
188	"	——	321	128	46	——	495
759	Dec	48	578	631	427	——	1684
760	"	880	537	520	412	——	2349
761	"	126	55	83	——	——	264
762	"	——	——	——	——	——	——
188	"	——	——	40	264	——	304

Note: "m" denotes a missing report sheet.

Total engine mileage run for twelve months, calculated from the available report sheets:

759	*Yeo*	11 months	20,997
760	*Exe*	9 months	19,617
761	*Taw*	11 months	14,699
762	*Lyn*	8 months	8,608
188	*Lew*	6 months	3,507
		Grand Total	67,428 miles run

1926

Engine	Date	a	b	c	d	e	Total
759	Jan	356	446	629	496	190	2117
760	"	624	455	362	568	367	2376
761	"	——	——	——	——	——	——
762	"	——	——	——	——	——	——
188	"	——	297	184	94	——	575
759	Feb	407	377	573	227	——	1584
760	"	714	319	270	——	——	1303
761	"	——	——	——	——	——	——
762	"	82	107	——	——	——	189
188	"	811	390	384	387	——	1972

759	Mar	733	516	546	466	——	2261
760	„	626	318	——	——	——	944
761	„	——	——	——	——	——	——
762	„	——	——	——	——	——	——
188	„	445	334	603	740	——	2122
759	Apl	431	588	600	316	——	1935
760	„	143	437	602	874	——	2056
761	„	——	——	——	16	——	16
762	„	40	——	——	——	——	40
188	„	452	180	——	359	——	991
759	May	——	——	497	125	——	622
760	„	215	199	618	447	——	1479
761	„	——	——	——	——	——	——
762	„	——	——	——	——	——	——
188	„	213	——	424	251	——	888

(No explanation is given to account for the low mileage run during this month.)

759	June	938	81	493	459	——	1971
760	„	155	595	585	619	——	1954
761	„	384	452	122	——	——	958
762	„	——	——	——	——	——	——
188	„	——	53	—123	——	176	352
759	July	364	204	269	809	——	1646
760	„	140	591	614	707	——	2052
761	„	289	50	234	934	——	1507
762	„	——	——	——	——	——	——
188	„	368	370	372	422	——	1532
759	Aug	39	——	209	425	–m–	673
760	„	364	665	718	525	–m–	2272
761	„	297	667	688	707	–m–	2359
762	„	58	——	——	40	–m–	98
188	„	296	699	587	537	–m–	2119
759	Sept	543	469	500	750	——	2262
760	„	560	458	466	——	——	1484
761	„	893	636	455	437	——	2421
762	„	234	——	42	53	——	329
188	„	344	429	144	124	——	1041

759	Oct	226	279	249	494	372	1620
760	„	—	—	—	—	—	—
761	„	547	618	370	—	—	1535
762	„	—	—	450	397	187	1034
188	„	248	262	81	251	—	842
759	Nov	—	—	251	399	—	650
760	„	—	—	—	—	—	—
761	„	821	581	374	226	—	2002
762	„	533	191	212	197	—	1133
188	„	382	376	460	147	—	1365
759	Dec	314	518	122	422	105	1481
760	„	—	—	—	—	—	—
761	„	574	292	263	432	247	1808
762	„	84	42	131	—	—	257
188	„	431	341	664	—	—	1436

Note: "m" denotes a missing report sheet

Total engine mileage run for twelve months, calculated from the available report sheets:

759	Yeo	12 months	18,822
760	Exe	9 months	15,920
761	Taw	8 months	12,606
762	Lyn	7 months	3,080
188	Lew	12 months	15,059
		Grand Total	65,487 miles run

1927

Engine	Date	a	b	c	d	e	Total
759	Jan	139	—	627	–m–	87	853
760	„	—	—	25	–m–	497	522
761	„	370	459	167	–m–	—	996
762	„	—	276	178	–m–	—	454
188	„	299	572	251	–m–	191	1313
759	Feb	–m–	—	334	—	—	334
760	„	472	420	437	495	—	1824
761	„	–m–	163	—	47	—	210
762	„	—	—	—	—	—	—
188	„	686	611	386	223	—	1906

759	Mar	–m–	–m–	——	——	——	——
760	,,	–m–	–m–	316	380	739	1435
761	,,	–m–	–m–	761	466	453	1680
762	,,	–m–	–m–	137	368	57	562
188	,,	–m–	–m–	——	——	125	125
759	Apl	——	——	——	——	——	——
760	,,	221	450	509	495	——	1675
761	,,	472	252	10	88	133	955
762	,,	57	43	90	418	183	791
188	,,	251	461	518	339	382	1951
759	May	——	——	——	——	24	24
760	,,	305	432	388	753	464	2342
761	,,	306	515	224	91	44	1180
762	,,	——	——	137	176	——	313
188	,,	——	420	416	340	458	1634
759	June	292	428	456	363	——	1539
760	,,	467	346	498	513	——	1824
761	,,	——	307	165	348	——	820
762	,,	74	——	210	337	——	621
188	,,	764	129	——	——	——	893
759	July	635	717	684	298	333	2667
760	,,	389	517	767	750	296	2719
761	,,	——	176	——	——	——	176
762	,,	128	113	——	389	39	669
188	,,	104	256	482	479	342	1663
759	Aug	1074	676	387	766	——	2903
760	,,	1022	834	518	558	——	2932
761	,,	130	——	641	427	——	1198
762	,,	224	166	——	——	——	390
188	,,	990	684	608	473	——	2755

Note: the exceptional mileage run during August, with a total of 10,178 engine miles.

759	Sept	777	564	771	380	——	2492
760	,,	637	764	727	315	——	2443
761	,,	225	131	——	——	——	356
762	,,	——	84	222	630	——	936
188	,,	521	367	231	667	——	1786

		a	b	c	d	e	Total
759	Oct	269	–m–	–m–	382	——	651
760	"	371	–m–	–m–	419	122	912
761	"	——	–m–	–m–	9	200	209
762	"	125	–m–	–m–	574	466	1165
188	"	90	–m–	–m–	——	——	90
759	Nov	242	589	754	603	——	2188
760	"	989	209	415	372	——	1985
761	"	——	275	——	——	——	275
762	"	365	132	——	195	——	692
188	"	——	——	——	——	——	——
759	Dec	230	279	752	688	——	1949
760	"	745	599	——	——	——	1344
761	"	——	——	——	——	——	——
762	"	195	295	47	366	——	903
188	"	——	——	391	897	——	1288

Note: "m" denotes a missing report sheet

Total engine mileage run for the twelve months, calculated from the available report sheets:

759	*Yeo*	10 months	15,600
760	*Exe*	12 months	21,957
761	*Taw*	11 months	8,055
762	*Lyn*	11 months	7,496
188	*Lew*	11 months	15,404
		Grand Total	68,512 miles run

1928

Engine	Date	a	b	c	d	e	Total
759	Jan	174	584	744	509	–m–	2011
760	"	——	——	——	——	–m–	——
761	"	——	——	16	79	–m–	95
762	"	59	241	103	89	–m–	492
188	"	372	597	315	539	–m–	1823

Note: "m" denotes a missing report sheet.

Appended are the official distances from end to end of the Line and between the centres of intermediate stations; they may help in appreciating the engine and train miles once run to schedule on this little railway; if an attempt is made to analyse any individual engine mileage for the day, week or month one or more of the following possibilities must be remembered and may fully account for other miles run over and above those allowed on the "out and home" journey:

a. empty coach working to and from Barnstaple and Pilton Yard
b. running round the train at termini
c. shunting movements at stations
d. extra and ballast train working
e. engine acting as "pilot" for whole or part distance
f. engine on "trial run" after overhaul or repair
g. engine used for breakdown purposes

	m	c	l		m
Barnstaple		37	57	Pilton	½
Pilton	2	54	56	Snapper	2¾
Snapper	4	54	83	Chelfham	4¾
Chelfham	7	54	2	Bratton	7¾
Bratton	11	62	45	Blackmoor	11¾
Blackmoor	14	33	63	Parracombe	14½
Parracombe	15	77	54	Woody Bay	16
Woody Bay	17	35	74	Caffyns	17½
Caffyns	19	23	18	Lynton	19¼

(*Chain Measure – 100 links: 1 chain – 80 chains: 1 mile*)

The "out and home" mileage allowance from Pilton Yard appears to vary between 39 and 45 thus giving an average of 42 miles; thus an engine taking two "out and home" turns per day and working a full six days will have a weekly total of 504 "miles run"; other higher and lower totals can similarly be examined and extracted.

CEY BROOK VIADUCT

Appendix Four

Stores Issue Book Quantities
(coal and oil)
1909, 1921, 1930 to 1934

Compiled by W.E. Hayward

Extracted and tabulated from the original Stores Book, parts of which were found among some débris at the old Pilton Depot in September, 1938.

Pre-Grouping – General Stores Requisitions

Date		*Month of November 1909*
15	Bray	1 gallon paraffin – 1 lb waste
16	Fitting shop	4 gallon paraffin – 2 gallons engine oil
17	Yard Box	2 gallon paraffin
24	Goods Dept.	1 gallon paraffin – 1 lb waste – 2 sponge cloths
3	Chelfham	6 gallon paraffin – 2 lbs waste – ½ ton coke
3	Bratton	2 gallon paraffin – 1 station hand truck
4	Blackmoor	24 gallon paraffin – ½ gallon colza oil – ½ gallon engine oil – 4 lbs waste – 1 packet Hudson's soap – 2 sheets emery cloth – 1 floor cloth – 1 packet toilet paper – ½ lb pumice dust – 1 ton coal
1	Woody Bay	8 gallon paraffin – 1 gallon colza oil – 2 sponge cloths – 1 floor cloth – 1 packet blacklead – 1 yard lampwick – 1 ton coal
2	Lynton	9 gallon paraffin – 2 lbs waste – 1 gallon colza oil – 1 packet blacklead

Date		*Month of December 1909*
10	Fitting shop	1 gallon paraffin – 1 gallon engine oil
11	Yard Box	3 gallon paraffin – 1 gallon colza oil – 2 lbs waste – 2 sponge cloths
27	Chelfham	6 gallon paraffin – 2 lbs waste – 2 check dusters – 2 signal lamps, repaired – 5 gallons paraffin
1	Bratton	5 gallon paraffin – 1 tin Glucoline – 2 yds lampwick – ½ ton coke
6	Blackmoor	12 gallons paraffin – 4 gallon colza oil – ½ gallon engine oil – ½ gallon cylinder oil – 4 lbs waste – 2 sponge cloths – 2 check dusters 2 sheets emery cloth – 1 packet blacklead – 1 hard broom – 10 gallons paraffin
1	Woody Bay	10 gallons paraffin – 3 Duplex lamp chimneys – 1 ton coal
1	Lynton	9 gallons paraffin – 1 gallon colza oil – 2 lbs waste – 1 gallon Jeye's fluid – 4 sponge cloths – 4 yds lampwick – 3 lamp chimneys – 1 packet blacklead – 1 blacklead brush – 1 shining brush – 2 lamps, repaired – 3 gallons paraffin – 6 tons coal

The previous items are interesting in showing the varied items that even a small railway has to make provision for in ordinary working; these details and those on the following 3 pages were taken from old, and very damp, bundles of papers found at the old Pilton Offices of the Company; when the Property was sold by Auction in October 1938 the Pilton premises were purchased by Mr J. Sanders, a previous tenant, for about £3,000.

For the Month of March 1921   (No Sunday Trains)

Name	Days	Coal	Eng. Oil	Cyl. Oil
Yeo	13	12.05 tons	67½ pts	28 pts
Exe	16	14.17 „	82½ „	42 „
Taw	19	17.03 „	102½ „	66 „
Lyn	7	6.06 „	48½ „	16 „
Carriage Oil				16 galls
Wagon Oil				10 „
Paraffin Oil		Cleaners		52 pts
		Fitting shop		3 galls
		Yard Box		2 „
		Bray		1 „
		Bratton		3 „
		Woody Bay		8 „
		Lynton		2 „
Colza Oil		Engine lamps		3 „
		Yard Box		1 „
		Bray		1 „
		Lynton		1 „

In Stock 31st March 1921

4 Casks of Engine Oil	P–964
2 Casks of Cylinder Oil	C–704
2 Casks of Dark Lubricating Oil	L. M.
1 Cask of Colza Oil	
3 Gallons of oil for Blackmoor engine	
20 Gallons of oil for Fitting shop engine	
¾ Cask of Grease	
¾ Cask of Tallow	
5 Bags of Waste	

For the Month of June 1921   *(No Sunday Trains)*

Name	Days	Coal	Eng. Oil	Cyl. Oil
Yeo	—	— tons	— pts	— pts
Exe	15	14.12 „	77½ „	40 „
Taw	19	18.18 „	97½ „	70 „
Lyn	20	19.19 „	107½ „	64 „
Carriage Oil				16 galls
Wagon Oil				11 „
Paraffin Oil		Cleaners		52 pts
		Blackmoor		40 galls
		Woody Bay		4 „
Colza Oil		Engine lamps		1 „
		Yard Box		1 „
		Lynton		1 „

In Stock 30th June 1921

2 Casks of Engine Oil	P–964
1 Cask of Cylinder Oil	C–704
1 Casks of Dark Lubricating Oil	L. M.
1 Cask of Colza Oil	
3 Gallons of oil for Blackmoor engine	
16 Gallons of oil for Fitting shop engine	
½ Cask of Grease	
¾ Cask of Tallow	
10 Bags of Waste	

For the Month of December 1921   *(No Sunday Trains)*

Name	Days	Coal	Eng. Oil	Cyl. Oil
Yeo	20	20.00 tons	105 pts	46 pts
Exe	—	— „	— „	— „
Taw	21	22.05 „	107½ „	78 „
Lyn	18	20.06 „	92½ „	52 „
Carriage Oil				16 galls
Wagon Oil				10 „
Paraffin Oil		Cleaners		54 pts
		Fitting shop		2 galls
		Yard Box		3 „
		Bray		1 „
		Chelfham		6 „
		Bratton		4 „
		Blackmoor		40 „
		Woody Bay		8 „
		Lynton		2 „

Colza Oil	Engine lamps	2 „
	Yard Box	1 „
	Bray	1 „
	Lynton	1 „

The Carriage and Wagon oil consumption would appear to be unduly high, and one might reasonably suppose that "gallons" had been substituted for "pints" but after careful examination of reports covering 15 months the figures are given under "gallons".

The Fitting shop had a large gas engine for driving the shafting and machine tools, and Blackmoor had an engine to drive the water pump.

Colza oil was, presumably used for the signal and hand lamps; the Pilton Yard Box would also have to supply the 4 lamps on the Pilton and Braunton road level crossing gates, but it is unknown why Pilton and Lynton only drew supplies of colza oil as the other stations all had an average of 4 signal lamps each.

If an engine was undergoing heavy repairs in the Fitting shop an issue of both Engine and Cylinder oil was made, additional to the above figures, for primary filling purposes.

Week ending: Wednesday 26th February, 1930

No.	Days	Coal	Eng. Oil	Cyl. Oil	Paraffin
188	6	4 tons	9½ pts	6 pts	2 pts
759	–	– „	– „	– „	– „
760	3	3¼ „	10 pts	6 pts	2 pts
761	6	4¾ „	15 „	10 „	4 „
762	5	6¼ „	18½ „	10 „	2 „

Week ending: Wednesday 10th August, 1932

No.	Days	Coal	Eng. Oil	Cyl. Oil	Paraffin
188	5	6½ tons	27½ pts	10 pts	2 pts
759	7	8 „	36 „	13 „	2 „
760	1	½ „	3½ pts	1 pts	pts
761	5	3½ „	14½ „	6 „	„
762	1	2½ „	10½ „	4 „	2 „

Week ending: Wednesday 8th August, 1934

No.	Days	Coal	Eng. Oil	Cyl. Oil	Paraffin
188	7	8¾ tons	37 pts	19 pts	1 pts
759	1	1½ „	6 „	3 „	½ „
760	5	7¼ „	28 „	15 pts	½ „
761	4	2½ „	16 „	6 „	1 „
762	2	1 „	3 „	1 „	„

Appendix Five

Traffic Reports 1901–1913

YEAR	PASSENGERS Receipts			GOODS (TONS) Carried	
	First	Third	Total	Mineral	General
1901	6,836	69,780	76,616	1,463	3,588
1902	6,910	75,953	82,863	2,810	5,095
1903	7,550	83,363	90,913	3,013	5,227
1904	6,869	82,231	89,100	2,763	4,402
1905	7,426	84,717	92,143	2,115	4,341
1906	7,535	87,126	94,661	3,022	4,692
1907	7,735	93,127	100,862	2,420	4,577
1908	6,989	91,745	98,734	2,860	4,636
1909	6,534	96,766	103,300	3,372	5,002
1910	6,333	96,806	103,139	3,089	4,929
1911	6,289	93,474	99,763	2,829	4,804
1912	5,461	93,906	99,367	3,216	4,856
1913	5,621	103,406	109,027	3,396	4,960